HOW DOES GOD GUIDE ? ? ?

Derek Tidball

ZondervanPublishingHouse
Grand Rapids, Michigan

A Division of HarperCollins*Publishers*

How Does God Guide?
Copyright © 1991 by Derek Tidball

Requests for information should be addressed to:
Zondervan Publishing House
1415 Lake Drive, S.E.
Grand Rapids, Michigan 49506

Library of Congress Cataloging-in-Publication Data

Tidball, Derek.
   How does God guide? / Derek Tidball.
     p. cm.
   ISBN 0-310-45661-4
   1. Christian life—1960- 2. Prayer—Christianity. 3. Wisdom—
Religious aspects—Christianity. I. Title.
BV4012.2.T63   1991
248.4—dc20   91–12096
                                              CIP

All Scripture quotations, unless otherwise noted, are taken from the *Holy Bible: New International Version* (North American Edition). Copyright © 1973, 1978, 1984 by the International Bible Society. Used by permission of Zondervan Bible Publishers.

Edited by Mary McCormick
Interior designed by Kim Koning
Cover designed by Mark Veldheer

Printed in the United States of America

91 92 93 94 95 96 / CH / 10 9 8 7 6 5 4 3 2 1

Contents

It's My Fault:
a personal explanation

God must have a sense of humor. No sooner had I turned my attention to preparing to write this book than invitations started to come our way. My wife and I were happily settled in the ministry of a church and we had no thought of leaving. We envisaged being there for several years to come. There was much work to be done. Then, suddenly, in the space of a month we were invited to consider several urgent (and some attractive!) invitations to ministry elsewhere, two or three of which came from the other side of the world. Other requests came, to undertake responsibilities that could go alongside our present work. But should we accept them? All these approaches required decisions.

My wife blamed it on me! If only I had not committed myself to write a book on guidance, we would not find ourselves in this whirlpool of uncertainty. God was obviously making us test out what we were teaching others. She was right—well, to some extent. I often find that God does test me in those very areas I am currently tackling in my teaching ministry in the church. So I have made a mental note to avoid some issues, such as suffering, by which I do not want to be tested since I am a natural coward. But my wife was only partly right, because we were continuously facing other decisions possibly not quite so earth-shattering but that were nonetheless significant. What about buying a secondhand car so that we were both mobile? What would she do following the completion of some of her responsibilities that were to end shortly? Decisions about work, family, finances, travel, and plenty else were facing us daily.

The truth is that we need guidance all the time—not just occasionally when the big questions come up. Searching for guidance is not one of those adolescent phases, like pimples on the face, you grow out of. Here we were, happily married and settled, and I, at least, sad to say, approaching middle age—and the questions of guidance were still high on our agendas.

I originally consented to write this book because I have spent much time in the past and even now, counseling others in the areas of guidance. When I was a Bible college professor, I dealt with admissions, thus much of my time was taken up with listening to people explain why they felt guided to study the Bible, often with a view to entering full-time Christian service. Happily, most often my colleagues and I were able to confirm their guidance, but every now and again we felt they had got it wrong. How did we decide that? Sometimes we were successful in persuading them that they had been misguided, but not always. In any case, none of us claimed infallibility. Those conversations often revealed some hair-raising ideas, which would have been laughable had they not been so dangerous, as to how people thought God had guided them. Clearly there was widespread confusion over guidance. People were muddled about it. Their beliefs and practices certainly didn't find a secure foundation in the Bible.

Now that I am back in the pastoral ministry, my fears have not lessened. There seems to be a general bewilderment made worse by the acceptance of some very unwise notions about how God guides. The confusion is aggravated by the fact that the traditional things preachers say about guidance often do not seem to work; at least, they do not work if one is honest.

Add to that the personal dimension and you can see why I felt that for my own sake if not for anyone else's, I should try to set out what the Bible does teach about guidance. It was time for a fresh look at how God guides.

The substance of this book was tested not only in our own lives but on my congregation at Mutley Baptist Church, Plymouth. The congregation is a real mixture of ages and experiences, but includes a larger number of students from the local Polytechnic and other colleges. I am grateful to them and equally to my older members for their contribution in writing this book. Many shared their own experiences with me, and were certainly not backward in asking awkward questions. Both the testimonies and the questions I found valuable. Many responded enthusiastically to the series I preached on guidance and encouraged me to think that I was talking biblical sense. I hope you find it so, too.

My prayer is that after reading this book you may be better equipped to discern the ways God uses to guide. I am not concerned that you should so much understand the theory (although I take the somewhat unfashionable view that theory matters) but that you may have a firmer grasp of the God who guides.□

Chapter 1

Are You Being Served?

It was a terrible evening. It was mid-November and very wet and very dark. I was driving with two friends from London to an isolated cottage in mid-Wales. I had only been there once before and it had been hard enough then for me to find it in the light. The cottage was situated seven miles from a Welsh town with an unpronounceable name, two miles from the nearest road up a farm track with several twists and turns and even more mini-crossroads in it. Between that road and the cottage lay seven farm gates, all of which had to be opened and carefully shut.

One of my friends was huddled in the passenger seat over a map that he was trying to read by courtesy of the dim glow of our interior light. It was obviously going to be a long and difficult journey. We were going to stay with friends who owned the cottage. Circumstances had dictated that they had to travel separately, and we did not expect to meet them on the road since they were supposed to have gone on ahead. But then, at the most difficult part of the journey, we were aware that the car behind was showing an unusual interest in us. After a few anxious moments, wondering if it was the police or someone with criminal intent, we realized that it was our friends' car. They had been delayed and were now behind us. Of course, we pulled aside and let them overtake us.

What a difference it made! They knew the way. It was their cottage and they had been there many times before in all sorts of weather conditions. So we put away our map, turned off the interior light, sat back, relaxed, and followed the leader. We enjoyed the rest of the journey, confident that our guides knew exactly where they were going. We soon discovered other advantages to this style of driving. Their headlights picked out all the details of that awkward road, including the unexpected roadworks, and the protruding hedges, well before we reached them. So we were prepared. What is more, being in front meant it was my friends who had to endure the howling gale and open those seven farm gates up to their home!

A PERSONAL GUIDE

It was then I understood something I had found hard to grasp before. I had always been told that God had promised to be our guide but that he had never promised to give us a map of our lives in advance. I was told that it was much better this way, but I could never understand why. Until that November evening I would have much preferred the map. Why did not God let me know the plan for my life for the next ten or twenty years and then let me get on with it? I am an organized and somewhat independent type, so I would have appreciated it if God had handed over the plans. It would have helped me to do some future planning myself, and I would be doing God a favor by unloading one job from his already enormous responsibilities. He would no longer have to worry about keeping an eye on me! I could not understand why it was better that he should promise to be with me as my personal guide. That night, however, the reason began to dawn on me: It was far superior and far less stressful to have a guide who knew the way than to have a map with goofballs trying to read it in the dark who didn't. It was obvious!

That experience put the promises of the Bible in a different light for me. They began to make sense. Among those promises were verses like these:

> I will instruct you and teach you in the way you should go; I will counsel you and watch over you.
>
> Psalm 32:8

> For this God is our God for ever and ever; he will be our guide even to the end.
>
> Psalm 48:14

> You guide me with your counsel, and afterward you will take me into glory.
>
> Psalm 73:24

> Whether you turn to the right or the left, your ears will hear a voice behind you saying, "This is the way; walk in it."
>
> Isaiah 30:21

> The LORD will guide you always; he will satisfy
> your needs in a sun-scorched land and will
> strengthen your frame.
>
> Isaiah 58:11

Now I know the value of the personal touch and I am sure that the most important thing any Christian can know about guidance is that God promises to guide us personally and that he is always true to his promises. He promises to be with us all the time as we face the choices and come to the crunch decisions.

Think of the implications of such a promise:

It means that there can be no slick formulas by which we can be sure we have got our guidance right. Relationships with living people, let alone with the living God, cannot be reduced to formulas or systems. When I take my car in for service, the garage runs down a checklist of factors to diagnose its state of health. Certainly I do not relate to my wife like that! Similarly, there is no easy checklist of factors that can readily assure us of the correct answers when it comes to guidance. Rather, as in all relationships, we are involved in a daily encounter and a developing bond that runs the whole spectrum of emotions and other factors involved in any kind of kinship.

It means that we are not guided automatically as though God has programmed us as we might program a computer. He is not impersonal in his dealing with us.

It means we have to use our minds and develop our relationship with God. We have an intelligent contribution to make, and God expects us to do so.

Above all, it means we can be sure of God's

personal interest in us. That has great advantages. We will never find ourselves in the uncomfortable position of the supposed passengers on the flight from London to New York who, a half hour after take-off, heard over the intercom, "Good morning, ladies and gentlemen. Welcome aboard the 7:30 A.M. flight from London to New York. This is a recording. You have the privilege of being on the first wholly automatic flight. There is no pilot, co-pilot, or flight engineer on board. We took off electronically and are now cruising at a height of 30,000 feet electronically, but don't worry. Nothing can go wrong, go wrong, go wrong, go wrong. . . . "

With God personally in control we can certainly be justified in feeling more secure.

EVIDENCE FROM EXPERIENCE:
THE OLD TESTAMENT

The Bible does not leave the matter there. In addition to the bold but unsupported claims it makes about God, it provides the testimony of God's people down through the years. One of the popular pictures they used when speaking of God was that of the shepherd. It captured something of what they had discovered about him. It spoke of the warm relationship that existed between God and his people and of his utter reliability. It summoned up a whole constellation of ideas about God as the one who fed, provided, protected, rescued, defended, nursed, and ruled the sheep. Being a guide was central to those ideas. Thus, Psalm 23, after asserting from personal experience that "The

LORD is my shepherd," naturally goes on to say, in verse 2 and 3, "He leads me beside quiet waters. . . . He guides me in paths of righteousness."

Centuries before, Jacob had spoken in very similar terms about God. At the end of his long life he bore witness to God as "the God who has been my shepherd all my life to this day" (Genesis 48:15). What a life his had been!

His home was one where argument and jealousy were rife. It had molded him into thinking that he was not going to get anywhere in life unless he constantly manipulated things to his own ends. He was the original Mr. Fix-It. His crafty scheming, however, only led him deeper into trouble. It caused a major rupture in his own family, which resulted in his being a fugitive from his home for many years. While on the run he married, but further difficult relationships with his father-in-law followed, and he set off on his journeys once more. Eventually he went home but did so in trembling and fear.

While he was en route home, God began to teach him some hard personal lessons. He was humbled enough by God to know that rather than fight for himself all the time, he should trust his life to God.

Once home, he was dogged by further unhappiness. Rachel, his wife, died giving birth to Benjamin. His father died. Then another favorite son, Joseph, disappeared under mysterious circumstances and was presumed dead. Years later, however, when Jacob and his large family were struggling with a disastrous famine, Joseph turned up again in Egypt, where he had become an important government official. So the frail and elderly Jacob, with all his family, relocated from Canaan to Goshen in Egypt, there finally to settle as a united family. It was perhaps the only time Jacob was truly happy in all his life.

Jacob had spent his life journeying from Beersheba to Haran and back again and then from Hebron to Egypt. The journeys had been marked more by darkness, accident, and folly than by prosperity and blessing, although he had known a measure of that, too. Yet, reflecting on it all, the most profound interpretation he could give to it was that God had been his guide. God guides not only when it is obvious that he is doing so because we are experiencing the joy of his blessing, but equally when darkness falls over our lives.

When we look at the rest of the Old Testament, this conviction that God guides remains strong. As the children of Israel wandered in the wilderness, God guided them by means of a pillar of cloud by day and a pillar of fire by night (Exodus 13:21). Moses confidently sang to God, "In your unfailing love you will lead the people you have redeemed. In your strength you will guide them to your holy dwelling" (Exodus 15:13).

This conviction was one from which God's people never digressed. The psalmists built their prayers on the assumption that God would guide them. Without it there was little point in praying. So, in Psalm 25:5 the psalmist prays, "Guide me in your truth and teach me, for you are God my Savior." Again, in Psalm 31:3, we read, "Since you are my rock and my fortress . . . lead and guide me."

Even when the national tragedy of the Exile occurred, when all seemed hopeless and the nation was all but obliterated, the prophets still asserted that God would guide them along the unfamiliar paths they were now compelled to tread (Isaiah 42:16) and that in the barren and thirsty desert God would have compassion on them and continue to show them the way (Isaiah 49:10). In view of all that they were going through, that was a remarkable assertion of faith. Many probably doubted whether God really was interested in them anymore, but the prophets were in no doubt and affirmed that even when they felt deserted, God remained their guide.

NEW UNDERSTANDING IN THE NEW TESTAMENT

At first sight, such outright assertions seem absent from the New Testament. Whenever the word "guide" is used in the New Testament, with only one exception, it is used in a quite ordinary sense of one person directing another to some earthly destination. Nonetheless, it is clear throughout the New Testament that his people were still conscious of God as their guide. Luke, for example, in his story of the early church quite frequently indicates that people experienced his guiding hand as, for instance, we see in Acts 8:29; 13:2; 15:28; and 16:6.

The New Testament Christians were no less aware that God was guiding them than were their Old Testament forerunners. The difference is that they attribute that guidance not so much to God himself as to the Holy Spirit. Their story is the story of the promise Jesus made in John 16:13—the only verse in the New Testament to use the word "guide" in the sense of God-given direction—working itself out in their lives. He promised, "When he, the Spirit of truth, comes, he will guide you into all truth."

It is an idea John develops in 1 John 2:20 and 27, where he indicates that every believer has the anointing of the Holy Spirit. Among the blessings that this anointing brings is the blessing that the Holy Spirit takes up residence within us to serve us as our continuous guide. He is no longer someone we visit on occasions of special need as we might return to an old schoolteacher whom we used to respect for advice about our careers. He lives within us and is permanently at hand. John writes this to encourage doubters to be more confident in their faith. Today we might confirmingly say that it should encourage confident believers to be sensitive in their decisions. The voice of the indwelling Spirit should be listened to and obeyed.

The cumulative evidence of Scripture, confirmed by the experience of believers down through the centuries, is that the Christian lives "a guided life." As J. I. Packer has written, "It is impossible to doubt that guidance is a reality intended for, and promised to, every child of God. Christians who miss it thereby show only that they did not seek it as they should. It is right therefore to be concerned about one's own receptiveness to guidance, to study how to seek it."

Few would dream of skiing down the snow-laden slopes of a Swiss mountain without an experienced guide close at hand to instruct and direct them. Nor should we go hurtling down the paths of life with all their potential hazards, avalanches, crevasses, and sudden storms without consciously submitting to the authority of the divine guide. Life can be as exhilarating as skiing—and as dangerous, too. A guide is needed and is ready at hand if we ask one to take charge of us.

Fine. So far we would all agree. There can surely be no dispute. Even if we doubt that God is guiding us when we are caught in the vortex of having to make pressurized decisions, most of us can see with the benefit of hindsight that God was with us, guiding us all the time.

The problem most of us face is not whether God guides us, but how.□

Chapter 2

Does It Work?

Few need to be convinced that finding guidance is important. For many it is like a chronic, gnawing toothache. It's uncomfortable and it won't go away. Should a young man marry Jane, or Mary? Or, should a young woman propose to Cedric, or Marmaduke? Or should we be traditional and wait for the other party to pop the question? Should we train to be an architect, an accountant, or a roadsweeper? Should we stay at school or leave? Should we accept this job or wait a few more days for another we hope to land? Should we buy a car and, if so, which one? Should we support this cause or that one? Should we follow the San Francisco '49ers or the Miami Dolphins?

CHOICES ... CHOICES

The questions are endless. They never seem to go away. Every time we think we have them dispersed, they have a nasty habit of popping up again. The reason is that the choices we face are far more numerous than those our grandparents faced. Never before have people lived in such an open society. Of course, we are not the first generation who have had to choose. From year zero in human history people have had to choose, as Adam and Eve learned with such disastrous consequences in the Garden of Eden. In fact, the ability to make choices and to take responsibility for those decisions is partly what distinguishes us from animals. It makes us human.

Yet, think of the trivial choices we make within the first thirty minutes of getting up in the morning. They are without precedent in human history. What are we going to choose to wear from our generous wardrobes? Which of the twenty-three breakfast cereals on sale in the average supermarket are we going to eat, if any at all? And, as we slurp our whatever in our half-awake state, which of the numerous daily newspapers are we going to read? Or don't we bother with the newspaper, choosing instead to watch the TV . . . or listen to the radio? We probably don't stop to seek much guidance over these choices or we'd never get out to work! But the choices are there and numerous nonetheless.

Elsewhere the choices are much more serious, as well as more numerous and more complicated than ever before. We are much more mobile than previous generations have been. It has been calculated that we meet in just one week as many people as a person in the Middle Ages would have met in a lifetime. Think of how that complicates things. Potential marriage partners, potential job opportunities, potential lifestyles are legion and we have to choose. No wonder we need guidance!

BUT THE QUESTION IS HOW?

Christians may be very eager to please God, but just how are they to find out what God wants them to do about the many areas of their lives about which the Bible does not give a direct and personally addressed answer?

Most of us have been taught that there are a number of ways God has given us to help us find out his will. Chief among these are:

Scripture

The advice of wiser Christians

Our inner feelings

Signs

Circumstances: open and closed doors

All we need to do is to line these up like landing lights on a runway, and, provided they are in order, we should be in for a safe landing. They will soon tell us what God's will is for us, and we can be confident that we're sticking to his plans for our lives.

There is certainly much value in each of these guidelines. The Christian who ignores them does so at his peril, but honesty compels us to admit that it is not that simple. Guidance does not usually work like that, or if it does, it does not always do so smoothly. Let's explore these ways God has given us to help us find out his will more fully, and look at some of the problems.

Scripture

The Bible itself claims that Scripture has a crucial role to play in providing us with guidance. Psalm 119:105 says, "Your word is a lamp to my feet and a light for my path." It seems as though the Bible can show us the way to go. And so it can. It can tell us the difference between right and wrong, between paths that are wise and those that are foolish. So many of the choices we face are, or should be, settled immediately by the Bible.

If we are considering asking God if we should steal, then we are wasting our time. The answer from God will clearly be, "No." His abhorrence of stealing is frequently mentioned in the Bible from Exodus 20:15 to Ephesians 4:28. If we are considering employment in a brothel, then the whole moral framework of the Bible from its condemnation of adultery to its positive exposition of the meaning of love should be sufficient to convince us to look for another job. If, as a convinced Christian, we are considering marrying an unbeliever, most Christians would agree that 2 Corinthians 6:14–7:1 advises us strongly against it even though it does not explicitly mention marriage.

Many Christians would go further and vouch for the fact that the Bible has guided them not just about the great moral choices they face but about the very personal decisions they faced. It was as though a verse from the Bible had leaped off the page and hit them between the eyes. This should not surprise us, since the Bible is God's living book through which he still speaks. It is not a dead textbook. He can make certain verses speak to us in unmistakable terms and apply them directly to our circumstances whenever he chooses.

This happened once to Dietrich Bonhoeffer, the German church leader of the war years. He was in the United States at the invitation of several professors and was wondering whether he should stay or return to his native Germany. He was reading 2 Timothy and came to chapter 4, verse 21 that in his version spoke of Paul's request to Timothy to "come before winter." In those days it was not a question of hopping on a plane and being home mere hours later. The journey involved a boat trip lasting several weeks. He took that verse to be God's guiding him, and so, on July 8, 1939, he sailed home. Two months later, war was declared and he was back among his people when they needed him. There he played a strategic, though tragic, role in opposing Hitler and strengthening the confessing church, for which he eventually paid with his life. Surely God had guided him.

The Bible often seems to relate to our exact circumstances and to answer directly our urgent questions. It seems to be no accident that we are reading particular verses at that particular time. I know, inasmuch as it has spoken to me like this.

Other friends of mine have been getting their guidance like this for years. So what is the problem?

To be precise, there are two problems. First, it does not always work like that. There are other occasions when we are desperate for guidance and searching the Bible with all our senses alerted for a direct word from God on some particular matter, but in vain. The Bible just seems silent. No answer seems to come, and the passages read seem to have no relevance.

Second, and more serious, this is not primarily how we should be reading our Bibles. It carries with it the danger that we read into the Bible the answers we want to find there and it fails to let the Bible speak for itself. Take a silly but actual example. A Christian in the United States was wondering whether to buy a new tent from a major department store called Sears Roebuck or from elsewhere, because the last one he bought there leaked. He was just about to leave for the store when he decided to read his Bible one more time. He opened it at Deuteronomy 14 and found in verse 5 that among the animals that Jews were permitted to eat was the "roe deer." That was enough. It was the confirmation he was seeking. God approved of the roebuck, and therefore, naturally he should purchase his tent from Sears Roebuck.

Silly? Yes, it is! But sadly, not uncommon. God's intention in causing Deuteronomy 14:5 to be in the Bible had nothing to do with the petty choice that that believer confronted centuries later. Nor was it God's subtle way of ensuring healthy profits for Sears Roebuck. Rather, it had much to do with health regulations for the children of Israel wandering in the desert, but this man was so preoccupied with his own horizons that he saw them everywhere—even where they did not exist.

That so often happens. We are praying so earnestly for guidance that we tend to read it into the Bible. We start identifying with particular Bible characters or events. We do so selectively, of course. On the basis that Philip the evangelist was once told to go south (Acts 8:26), a friend of mine felt it right to move from the north and accept an attractive job in the south of England. He did not seem too pleased when I pointed out that Philip had been instructed to go to a desert and I wondered if my friend was prepared for that!

To be truthful, when we obtain guidance like that we are often reading into the Bible exactly what we want to see there. It is not insignificant that the guidance often comes from just half a verse and we ignore the other half, or from just one verse in a whole paragraph and we turn a blind eye to the rest.

Scripture may well speak to us like this, but it should not be the primary way we listen to the Bible's message. First and foremost we should be asking what the author intended his original readers to understand: what doctrines or principles it was first designed to teach. Only then are we able to make the jump across the centuries and apply it sensibly to our own lives today. It is, of course, much harder to read it this way than to look for the instant answers some of us have come to expect, but it is a great deal safer in the long run and considerably more mature as well.

The Bible is not a gigantic computer that can

spew out all the answers to our personal and particular questions at the touch of a button—"Is it Jane or Mary, accountancy or architecture?" It simply is not written that way. According to 2 Timothy 3:16, it is written to train us rigorously and equip us thoroughly so that we might live rightly. Part of that right living must include the ability to make wise decisions when choices confront us and guidance is needed.

Therefore, Scripture has a vital part to play in guidance, but maybe it is not the part we often assign to it.

The Advice of Others

The wise man in Proverbs has no doubt about the matter. If we are to come to sensible conclusions, we need an abundance of counselors. In Proverbs 15:22 he says: "Plans fail for lack of counsel, but with many advisers they succeed," and someone has translated Proverbs 11:14 as: "Where there is no guidance a people falls; but in an abundance of counselors there is safety" (RSV).

I know now what he means. Two young people fall desperately in love with each other, do not listen to anyone else's advice, rush headlong into marriage, and it proves a disaster. Everybody else could have told them it was a mistake from the beginning, but they did not ask and even if they had asked, they would not have listened. The author of Proverbs rightly warns us against not taking advice, or taking it only from a few yes-men who will only tell us what we want to hear.

We need to check our guidance with mature Christians who will be objective and frank with us, not just with the few who lack experience and will simply flatter us.

Yet there is another side to the coin, which the author of Proverbs does not seem to have considered. Perhaps I have been unfortunate, but if I have been, then so have many others. If I were writing some of his wise sayings, I would want to balance his comments with a proverb like, "In the abundance of counselors is confusion," or, "When guidance is needed do not ask too many others, as that path goes around in circles." The more people we ask, the more confused we become because often, but thankfully not always, they offer different and contradictory advice that ends up canceling itself. The danger is that ultimately we are either paralyzed into indecision or find ourselves doing exactly what we had made up our minds to do in the first place.

This is a real problem for many. I know one woman who packed her suitcase to go into a hospital for an operation and unpacked it again three times before finally calling off the operation. She did so because she was sure that the Lord must be speaking to her through whomever she had last spoken to. So, one friend said, "Go ahead" and the next said, "I wouldn't, if I were you." Another said, "It's essential," while the next said, "It really isn't necessary." Another friend said, "I had it done; it was worth it." Yet, another friend warned, "It didn't do any good for me. It just caused me a load of trouble." Whom was she to listen to?

As a basic principle the Bible teaches that, "God is not a God of disorder but of peace" (1 Corinthians 14:33). If this is what he is like, God obviously will not wish to keep his children in a whirl of confusion, spinning first this way, then that, getting dizzier and dizzier. So what are we to do?

First, we must pick our advisers wisely, going to those who know us well and know the situation well enough to give sensible advice. They should be people who are both mature and honest with us. Second, we should make them few. Certainly we need to hear more than one piece of advice about major decisions. The book of Proverbs is right. Some people will see some things, others will not. From several advisers we should be able to get a complete, or at least a rounded, picture. Third, having taken advice, we should decide and not be shaken from that decision unless some new piece of information of earth-shattering proportions is brought to our attention.

Furthermore, we really need to know ourselves. The problem with receiving advice from others is that it strikes us differently depending on who we are and according to our individual personalities. On the one hand, the confident, decisive person would probably benefit from listening more to the advice of others. On the other hand, those who are naturally diffident and hesitant probably ask for too much advice and suffer acutely when the advice they receive is confusing. They may even secretly welcome the confusion because it justifies their unwillingness to make a decision. Such people need to learn to take responsibility and to become the mature adults that Christ wants them to be.

Inner Feelings

The most popular method of guidance these days seems to be to appeal to our feelings. I am frequently told, "After I decided on this course of action, I felt peace about it." That seems to settle the matter. In the mind of those who speak like this, it means it must be right.

Some knowledgeable types even justify this approach by reference to a verse of Scripture. They quote Colossians 3:15, "Let the peace of Christ rule in your hearts, since as members of one body you were called to peace. And be thankful." They argue from this verse that they must be in the will of God if they have peace, because that is what they were called to. They sometimes even go further and tell me the word for "rule" is our word "umpire," so it has particular reference to making decisions and choosing between difficult alternatives. Because of this verse, they say, we must go for the decision that gives us peace.

In spite of such passionate argument, I must insist that a large warning sign with flashing red lights be erected over this path to guidance. Be careful! You are in danger of being misled! Let me set out my fears.

To begin with, quoting Colossians 3:15 is almost a complete red herring. The verse is not about guidance at all, as anyone can see if he carefully reads the full verse—and even more, its context. This verse is about relationships within the church. Paul is telling the Christians at Colosse that, like it or not, they have got to get on with each other and stop falling out with each other, because harmonious relationships are not irrelevant to but integral to the gospel they profess to believe. The verses that come immediately before are all about patience, forgiveness, love, humility, unity, and other such uncomfortable and demanding things. The verses that follow are about learning to live together at home and at work in a way pleasing to God. So it is in their relationships with one another that they should let peace be their umpire.

That is why I was careful to point out that this verse has *almost* nothing to say about guidance. It does have some bearing on the subject since it instructs us on how we should be guided to sort out disputes and arguments in the fellowship—by letting peace rule, but it has nothing to do with seeking guidance for individual matters or simply finding peace for ourselves.

Having dealt with the red herring, there is a deeper issue that needs to be examined: The question is, where does it teach us in the Bible that we will be sure that we have got the right answer about something when we feel peace about it? The answer is, nowhere. This principle does not come from the Bible at all. It is one we have picked up from our secular environment, which is contaminated with a philosophy called *existentialism*. This philosophy puts personal feelings at the center of attention. It argues, in many forms at least, that there are no rights or wrongs and no objective standards. It is subjective feeling that is to govern us. It says, "Do what makes you feel good"—a far cry from the teaching of the Bible.

A moment's thought will lead us to the conclusion that peace is never a major criterion for discerning guidance in the Bible. Moses felt no peace about going back to Egypt to set the Israelites free. Yet it was right that he went. Jeremiah certainly never felt at peace about his prophetic ministry. He spent all his time kicking and screaming about it, yet there is no doubt that God had surely called him to it and used him in it. Paul probably felt little peace when being flogged, imprisoned, or shipwrecked, but he was sure his missionary journeys were in the will of God. Above all, Jesus did not have this sublime sense of peace that many of us seem to expect when in the Garden of Gethsemane, yet never has a person been more submissive to the will of God than he was at that moment.

In the complacent luxury of our Christian living in the Western world we may believe that we can decide questions of guidance on the basis of whether we feel at peace about them or not. Many in our world cannot afford that luxury and have no such advantages if they are to be true to Christ. The Christian who goes to prison for his faith, or whose house is frequently searched, or who loses his job, or who has his family torn from him, or who is made the subject of vile lies or the target of a police frame-up because he follows Christ, may not be bathed in the imperturbable sense of equanimity we call *peace*. There are some outstanding testimonies of those who have felt at peace in such circumstances, but it is not always thus. Many know the struggles and turmoil that Paul writes of so movingly in 2 Corinthians. Yet, these believers are in the will of God. They have been guided to share in the sufferings of Christ and they accept it as the path they must tread.

We must be careful that our easy circumstances do not lead us to insult our suffering brothers and sisters elsewhere. Their experience calls into question the idea that peace settles matters of guidance. Inasmuch as we do not find it taught as a major principle within the Bible, in our eagerness to find guidance we must be cautious about erecting it to too prominent a position.

Signs

On some occasions, people in the Bible who were looking for guidance asked for a sign. Abraham's servant did (Genesis 24:12–14), when seeking a wife for Isaac. Gideon is perhaps the best-known example of someone who did so (Judges 6:36–40). He asked God to soak a fleece of wool he had left on the ground overnight while leaving the ground dry and then to reverse the trick the next night by soaking the ground while leaving the fleece dry. Should we not seek for signs?

At one stage in my life I was considering an invitation from a church to become their pastor. We will call it Lingmere Evangelical Fellowship. While the request was high on our prayer agenda, three signs occurred that suggested we should accept. A letter came from their previous pastor about something else

31

entirely. He was not a man with whom we had had or expected any contact. A friend who knew nothing of the situation mentioned it to us and suggested we might be suitable. Most remarkable of all, we had got a book out of our library on inter-library loan and on virtually every other page was stamped "Return to Lingmere." What more evidence could we possibly want than that? Nevertheless, we turned the invitation down, convinced on other and more important grounds than these signs that it was not right to accept. All the signs did not outweigh our careful thought about the matter.

In fact, the Bible gives us only a few examples of people being guided by signs and it does not seem to come highly recommended as a method of finding guidance. It is not really difficult to understand why. Honesty compels us to admit that we can usually find the sign we are looking for; that signs can be read several ways at once; that our minds play tricks on us, and that such signs often trivialize profound issues and vice versa.

When teaching at the London Bible College, I used to hear it all. An applicant knew that God had guided her to our particular college because she saw a pile of bricks with "LBC" inscribed on them. I myself felt that if she derived any guidance from those bricks it should probably have been to apply for a position at the London Brick Company that manufactured them and inscribed their initials on millions of them. Failing that, perhaps she would like to try the London Broadcasting Company. Why us?

Another, whom we had rejected, was quite sure

we had got it wrong. He told me his guidance was very definite and that he could not possibly have made a mistake. When I asked him what it was, he informed me that while going home from the interview on the bus he had seen the street name "Green Lane" as he entered the village where he lived. The college was situated in another "Green Lane," and the fact that his attention had been drawn to this name could not be a coincidence. To him it must have meant that God was saying, "Study at London Bible College." It could mean no other. The fact that "Green Lane" must be one of the most common street names in all England seemed to have eluded him. On other grounds, I remained firmly convinced that we had made the right decision.

Still another young man was convinced that God was calling him to work in Turkey. When asked why, he replied by saying that everywhere he went he saw "Turkish Delight" and he took this as a sign from God! His wise friends pointed out to him that it was just as well that he had not seen "Mars Bars" everywhere he went or else he would really have trouble with his guidance. Perhaps he would end up as the first interplanetary missionary! One could not help feeling, however, that he might not have much of an audience.

I know of one missionary now overseas whose calling was confirmed by her picking up a tea towel on which was printed the name of the society and the country where she now works. For her it was the final straw, confirming all that God had been saying in other ways. Undeniably, signs *may* be significant, but for the most part . . .

Beware of signs!

Circumstances: Open and Closed Doors

Surely circumstances are a much more reliable method of guidance. To avoid unnecessary generalizations, let us narrow our discussion to one particular set of circumstances—that of open and closed doors.

There would seem to be good biblical precedent for talking in these terms. The phrase "open door" certainly comes from the Bible and can be found, for example, in 1 Corinthians 16:9; 2 Corinthians 2:12; Colossians 4:3; and Revelation 3:8. Each time the Bible uses the phrase, it refers to an opportunity God has provided and expects his servants to seize with both hands.

It is true that the opportunity is always one for evangelism or mission, but surely it is a legitimate extension of the idea for Christians to talk about "open doors" in relation to other things as well. Consequently, the idea has been extended, and now "open" and "closed" doors are considered a regular factor in obtaining guidance. If God opens the door for us to accept a certain job, we should accept it; if the door is closed, then we will accept that it was not his will for us.

It is often our wider circumstances that determine whether the door is open or closed. Our mother-in-law is terminally ill, so the door seems closed to going to the mission field just now. The needs of our children prevent us from moving just now and so we cannot accept that new job. We have come to the end of one appointment and another comes along just at that moment, so we assume it must be God's will to do it.

It all seems straightforward enough. So what is the problem? The trouble is that in reality life is a little more complicated than our illustrations suggest. Sometimes the guidance is as simple as that, but not always.

The problem with open doors is that very often we face more than one open door at once. Then we have to decide which one God wants us to go through. Even if we only have one open door facing us at any one stage, it is not unlikely that we would be able to find a few more open doors if we wait a week or two. Besides, does it mean that it is right to go through every open door we face?

Likewise, closed doors also present problems. We have to decide whether a closed door is God saying a definite no to that avenue or whether he is just testing our commitment and determination. A friend of mine was sure she had been called by God to be a missionary nurse, but she failed her nursing examinations. Was that God saying she had got her guidance wrong or was he saying that he was toughening her up so that she would also be trained to face many disappointments in her future work for him? Was he, in fact, using the failure to teach her much about herself? I have known others who were convinced that God had called them to the ministry, but their denomination's selection conference has turned them down. Does that mean they got the call wrong, or that God was nudging them in the direction of getting further training or entering full-time Christian work through a different route? You are sure you should marry Cynthia, but she thinks differently about it. In fact, she will not even go out with you! The door seems firmly closed. Is it? Perhaps you just need to learn how to ask her properly rather than to approach her with all the arrogance of a male chauvinist under the delusion that she will want nothing better than you.

Thus, in practice, open and closed doors do not make guidance an open-and-shut case. They are never the final answers in matters of guidance. Even when we face them, we are left with the need to use our minds and to accept responsibility for the decisions we have reached.

CONCLUSION

Each of the approaches to guidance we have examined has presented us with problems. Helpful as they may be, none of them is unambiguous and clear. Line them up with each other and we still have problems since they often seem to contradict each other. The Bible seems to be saying one thing and circumstances another. All the advice we receive says to go ahead, but the door seems not only shut but bolted and locked. No wonder many find guidance such a problem.

Perhaps the problem does not lie so much in these means of guidance in themselves, since surely they all have something to offer and we would ignore them at our peril. Rather, perhaps the problem lies in some of the assumptions we hold that underlie our use of these methods of guidance. Perhaps we need to think more deeply about what we are expecting God to do and the way we are expecting God to work. Just what do we mean when we talk about God's will for our life?□

Chapter 3

What Is the Will of God?

David and Jennifer wrote to me recently, "We both feel God has a special purpose in bringing us together. The question is, 'What is it?'"

Virtually in the same mail delivery I received a letter from Julie, who wrote, "The more I prayed, the more crazy things seemed to get. It really is frustrating when you really want to know the will of God for your life and yet you don't hear anything."

Pastors are continually on the receiving end of such questions from people who are totally committed to Jesus Christ as the Lord of their lives but are struggling to find out what he wants them to do. The usual means of guidance, discussed in the previous chapter, have often been tried and found wanting. The answers seem elusive. As one college chaplain voiced it, "Was I out when God rang to give me the call, and did I fail to leave the answering machine on?" The question is asked so frequently that it suggests that it is time to step back a bit and take a fresh look at guidance.

Most of us make an assumption as we look for guidance. The assumption is that God has a will for our lives. By that we mean that God has a particular plan mapped out for our lives that details all the major decisions we will ever face, such as what job we should do; whether and whom we should marry; where we should live; when we should move on; which church we should join, and so on. Given that, it is still our responsibility to determine which way God wants us to go at each vital junction in our lives. At all major crossroads we must stop and ask whether we should turn right, left, or just go straight on. Our task as committed Christians is to discover what God has drawn on the map.

We hardly ever question whether this is a valid picture of the way God operates in our lives, since we know that the Bible frequently talks about "the will of God"—a phrase that we also know means what God wants or what pleases him. To be sure, the Bible is full of references to the will of God, but maybe it would be helpful to look carefully at just how the Bible uses this phrase before we jump to the conclusion that it contains the idea that God has just one particular plan for us that it is our duty to discover and obey, hard as it may be.

What does the Bible teach about "the will of God"?

GOD'S SOVEREIGN WILL

The Bible talks of God's will in two ways. The first way is in the sense of his sovereign will. This refers to the fact that God reigns supreme over everything; consequently, what he wants to happen will happen. Nothing can stand in his way.

David was conscious of God's having ultimate control in this way. Whether it was his successful desire to bring the Ark of the Covenant to Jerusalem, or his unsuccessful request to build the temple, he was deeply aware that it was God's will that would be done and not his personal plans that would be fulfilled (1 Chronicles 13:2; 2 Samuel 7:21).

This idea of God's sovereign will is brought into sharp focus when the Bible speaks about the death of Jesus. What happened in the crucifixion was neither a mistake, nor a man-made plan, but the will of the Lord. It was God's surprising way of bringing about our salvation. Both the prophet Isaiah (53:10) and the apostle Peter (Acts 4:38) spoke of God bringing to pass what he chose to do through that event rather than its being the mere outworking of human decisions. Onlookers may have thought that God had lost control of events. It certainly *seemed* that way, but nothing could have been further from the truth.

This teaching crops up in various forms throughout the Bible. Think of the following verses:

> Our God is in heaven;
> he does whatever pleases him.
>
> Psalm 115:3

> The LORD does whatever pleases him,
> in the heavens and on the earth,
> in the seas and all their depths.
>
> Psalm 135:6

The lot is cast into the lap,
but its every decision is from the LORD.

Proverbs 16:33

His dominion is an eternal dominion;
his kingdom endures
from generation to generation.
All the peoples of the earth
are regarded as nothing.
He does as he pleases
with the powers of heaven
and the peoples of the earth.
No one can hold back his hand
or say to him: "What have you done?"

Daniel 4:34–35

For nothing is impossible with God.

Luke 1:37

Think what this means. It means that what God wants to happen will happen and, conversely, that when things happen God's sovereign will has been accomplished. God brings to pass whatever he wills.

As soon as we hear such a claim, many of us want to protest and question God. It makes us sound devoid of human responsibility, and we do not like it. It seems to devalue us. Such questions are not new. Paul voices them in Romans 9:19 when he counters the idea that if God is in such control we, his people, are mere puppets on a string and cannot be held responsible for anything. He shows how foolish such a position is since we are God's creation and understand so little that we have no right to question God.

Still the questions come. If he is so powerful, why

does he tolerate suffering and put up with evil? Why did he permit this—or plan that? We naturally want to bring our own bewildering experiences to God and ask him for an explanation. But, alas, we shall find that many of these questions will ultimately remain unanswered this side of heaven.

Yet, while not pretending to know all the answers to hardship and suffering, we can put forward a few clues to help us understand their value. Sometimes when God denies us something we would clearly wish, he does so out of his providential love for us. He can see the way ahead more clearly than we can and knows that not all we want is good for us. Sometimes it is an act of discipline on his part, intended to bring us back into line with him or to encourage us to let go of unworthy things and walk more closely with him. Sometimes suffering comes and evil strikes to bring greater qualities out of our life that a life of ease would not otherwise achieve. Sometimes it is simply that we are victims of a less than perfect, indeed fallen, world and we simply suffer as many others do because we are subject to a creation that is and always will be groaning in travail and pain until Christ delivers it.

In spite of these explanations, however, there remain deep mysteries we may never understand. We must content ourselves with the knowledge that God is good as well as all-powerful, and although his sovereign will may seem a muddle to us, it is not unnecessary and it makes sense to him. Isaiah put his finger on it when he said, " 'For my thoughts are not your thoughts, neither are your ways my ways,' declares the LORD. 'As the heavens are higher than the earth, so are my ways higher than your ways and my thoughts than your thoughts'" (Isaiah 55:8–9).

Endless illustrations from human experience teach us that so often what looks like a mess can make perfect sense from a different perspective. The wrong side of some knitwear may appear to be a jumble and you may wonder why, until you turn it around and see the effect it has had in producing a beautiful, intricately crafted pattern on the side you are meant to see. Streets and buildings may look haphazard and without any plan until you are lifted above them in an airplane and see the design. A maze may be just that—a frustrating trap—until you see its skilled design from above and just how easy it really was to find your way out.

In protesting, as Job did, that the sovereignty of God seems hard to understand and we do not want to accept it, we are just revealing our humanness. Instead of protesting, however, we need to learn to think of the benefits we derive from God's sovereignty. If God is sovereign, it means that in the end he will override all opposition to him. Darkness, death, disease, hatred, demons, oppression, unrighteousness, whatever it is that is opposed to God, will ultimately be defeated. If he is sovereign, even things that are in opposition to his holy character but are nonetheless permitted by him can be turned to his own ends and made to serve his purposes.

Furthermore, his sovereignty means that even my inability to hear God's direction for my life, even my failures, my refusals, my stubbornness, and my wickedness cannot stand in God's way. He will bring out of my life what he wants and will use it as a way of bringing glory to his own name. I am not able to restrict God. This is what Paul meant when he said, "And we know that in all things God works for the good of those who love him, who have been called according to his purpose" (Romans 8:28). The "all things" not only includes the accidents, illnesses, and disappointments we usually think of when we quote this verse but our mistakes, failures, and disobediences as well. God cannot be thwarted. As R. C. Sproul, an American Bible teacher and theological lecturer, has written, "When he decrees something sovereignly, it will come to pass—whether I like it or not, whether I choose it or not. He is sovereign. I am subordinate."

Here, then, is a great comfort for every believer. Although God's will may be hidden and mysterious, it ultimately cannot be missed. That should not make us indifferent to seeking to discover his will, but it should take away the panic and stress that many subject themselves to and it should cause the fearful to trust him more. He is quite capable of coping with the situation even if we do turn the wrong corner on that map we think he has drawn for us, and he is also quite capable of making sure we do no such thing in the first place! What he wants us to do, we will do.

There is no more telling example of this in the Bible than Joseph. For years his family had been riddled with problems as well as blessings, and eventually they were worked out between Joseph and his older brothers. There were faults on both sides. The Bible never makes him out to have been a saint. When he was a child, he was a precocious brat. He must have been difficult to live with. Yet, neither does it justify the terrible steps taken by his brothers when they sold him into slavery in Egypt and pretended to his father that he was dead. The end result you know. By that curious route, which must have crushed his father's heart with grief, his brothers' hearts with guilt, and his own heart with confusion and anger, God arranged for him to become the chief minister of Egypt at a time of national crisis. Joseph was the deepest thinker of them all, and when they all met up again, his brothers were in fear and trembling lest he should hold a grudge against them. He said to them, "Don't be afraid ... You intended to harm me, but God intended it for good to accomplish what is now being done, the saving of many lives" (Genesis 50:19–20). There is the sovereignty of God at work.

GOD'S MORAL WILL

The second way in which the Bible clearly talks about the will of God is in the sense of how God wishes us to live morally and spiritually. In this respect the will of God—that is, what is right for us—has to do with the working out of our salvation and our growth in holiness. Paul said as much in Philippians 2:12 and 13. "Continue to work out your salvation with fear and trembling, for it is God who works in you to will and to act according to his good purpose."

The sovereign will of God may often be hidden from us. When it is, we should not spend time trying to guess what it is. This is idle speculation.

Rather, we should go on living in the way that God has already made plain that he wants us to. As Deuteronomy 29:29 puts it, "The secret things belong to the Lord but the things revealed belong to us and to our children, *that we may follow all the words of this law"* (italics mine).

God has revealed to us how we should live, not in the sense of whether we should live in Festiniog or Felixstowe, but in the sense that we should love not hate, be truthful not deceitful, be patient not quick-tempered, be humble not arrogant, be pure not immoral, and be forgiving not resentful. So much of the will of God is plain for all to follow.

It is this moral will of God that the authors of Scripture had in mind when they wrote verses like the following:

I desire to do your will, O my God;
your law is within my heart.

Psalm 40:8

Teach me to do your will, for you are my God;
may your good Spirit lead me on level ground.

Psalm 143:10

Trust in the LORD with all your heart
and lean not on your own understanding;
in all your ways acknowledge him,
and he will make your paths straight.

Proverbs 3:5–6

Whether you turn to the right or to the left, your ears will hear a voice behind you, saying, "This is the way; walk in it."

Isaiah 30:21

Your will be done on earth as it is in heaven.

Matthew 6:10

Whoever does God's will is my brother and sister and mother.

Mark 3:35

Therefore do not be foolish, but understand what the Lord's will is.

Ephesians 5:17

For this reason, since the day we heard about you, we have not stopped praying for you and asking God to fill you with the knowledge of his will through all spiritual wisdom and understanding.

Colossians 1:9

Epaphras ... is always wrestling in prayer for you, that you may stand firm in all the will of God, mature and fully assured.

Colossians 4:12

It is God's will that you should be sanctified.

1 Thessalonians 4:3

We often apply these verses to finding out God's individual will for our lives or to plotting God's map for our lives. We turn to them when we are wondering whether to buy a new stereo or apply for a particular job, but we ought to be able to see that they are not really about such questions. They are primarily about ethical, moral, and spiritual issues.

A further look at the context in which these verses are set confirms that they are about the moral, not individual, will of God. Look again, for example, at Psalm 40:8. There, doing God's will is clearly equated with obeying God's law. Or observe how 1 Thessalonians 4:3 continues. Having spoken about the will of God, it now illustrates or defines what that will is by reference to avoiding sexual immorality. So it is with them all. The will of God in these verses refers to the difference between good and bad, right and wrong, holiness and sin.

Exactly the same is true of the phrase "led by the Spirit," which occurs in Romans 8:14 and Galatians 5:18. These verses refer to the Spirit leading us to holiness, not really to being guided by him to a particular type of car we wish to buy or a career we may want to enter.

Of course, all these verses may have a spin-off effect on what we spend or on what job we do. Such decisions involve moral and ethical judgments. To live according to the revealed moral will of God will certainly limit excessive and selfish expenditure or point us in certain directions job-wise, ruling out those that are immoral or socially destructive. But we are wrong to apply these verses to such matters directly as we are in the habit of doing. That is to misunderstand them. They are about God's desire for us to be holy.

ALMOST A DIGRESSION, BUT NOT QUITE

Before we leave our discussion of God's moral will, we ought to make a slight digression and develop an issue raised earlier when we were looking at Scripture. There is one piece of debris that often seems to litter the landscape when Christians are seeking guidance. Not infrequently we find Christians looking for guidance when they should not be doing so. I refer to times when the Bible has already made clear God's will on a matter. When this occurs, we confront open-and-shut cases and we should not loiter near God, asking for guidance with the intent that he should change his mind.

I know some Christians who spend a long time praying about whether or not they should evangelize. Now there may be questions they should face as to how they should do so, but whether they should do so should never be questioned. Jesus made it clear that all of his disciples were to be involved in the great task of evangelism. Look at Matthew 28:19–20; John 20:21; and Acts 1:8 if you doubt it. Not only did the early church show by their example that they understood this to be an obligation laid on all believers but they continued to teach it as such—see Romans 10:9 and 1 Peter 3:15.

Therefore, let us not waste God's time nor our own, asking what his will is about this or that when he has already plainly spoken. When it comes to the need for honesty, for sexual fidelity in marriage, for integrity in the marketplace, for self-discipline in regard to eating and drinking, the need to speak graciously ... and a host of other issues, God has spoken. All we need to do is to obey.

Similarly, there are many things God has already declared to be wrong—thus, it is pointless to seek his approval for them in the hope that he will guide us to do them. Committing adultery or causing the break-up of another's marriage, developing a homosexual relationship that admits physical expression, plotting mischief or murder, picking a winner in order to live off the fruits of gambling and never have to work again are not matters that should detain us. Yet, to my certain knowledge, some Christians have prayed about such matters and sought to discover whether God would guide them into such a course of action.

There are other issues through which we know in a general way what God's moral will is, but we need to discern its particular application to us. Examine divorce, for example. We know that in general terms it is wrong and that God has declared in forceful language that he hates it (Malachi 2:16). However, we also know that there are some limited grounds on which it is acceptable (Matthew 19:9; 1 Corinthians 7:15), and it is legitimate therefore to pray as to what one might do if one finds oneself in those situations. Nevertheless, our praying must always take place within the limits laid down by the moral will of God. Therefore, the moral will of God gives us a basis on which we have to build an individual application. The fact that permission to divorce is given in these circumstances does not mean to say we have to choose that option.

Yet, are there not other situations in which the Bible seems to condone the breaking of a clear principle, and may it not occasionally be right for me to do so as well? If so, surely these are the very issues with which I am likely to spend time seeking guidance. In the Bible, for example, one thinks of Rahab telling lies to protect the Israelite spies she was hiding in her house (Joshua 2). In more recent history one thinks of the plot to kill Hitler, which, if successful, might have saved Europe from much further bloodshed. Should we not sometimes pray for guidance in such circumstances?

The answer is certainly, yes, but we need to qualify it. The first qualification is that such circumstances are usually extreme and the likes of you and me are probably not going to confront them much, if at all.

The second qualification is that we note in both preceding examples that the person did wrong in order to prevent a greater evil from being committed. It is important to notice that *it remains evil even if good comes out of it.* William Barclay helpfully commented some years ago that it is a bit like poison. Poison has sometimes a useful role to play in healing an infected body, but it remains poison nonetheless and the bottle should always be clearly labeled as such and kept in a locked cabinet.

For most of us such interesting questions are simply diversions—entertaining speculation about hypothetical situations—and nothing more. What we need is usually not more guidance in these areas but more obedience. That is why there are whole areas where the best advice is, "Don't think about it." If God says, "Do it," we should do it. If he says, "Don't do it," it should not even cross our minds to do it.

HIS INDIVIDUAL WILL

With that background we come now to ask what the Bible has to say about the will of God in the third sense, which is the sense of God's having an individual plan for our lives that it is our duty to discover.

Most Christians live as though God has such a plan and believe that what they have to do is to interpret the signs, to listen to Scripture, to take advice, and to be led by the inner senses until they can be sure that they have discovered what God wants them to do at each significant crossroad of their lives. In practice, as we have seen, it can be a highly unsettling experience. Not only are the signs far from simple in themselves but sometimes there seem to be no signs at all. At other times it almost seems as though God is playing some game of hide-and-seek with us. We think we have just arrived at a solution, then it all falls apart and we are back at the beginning! Such frustrations do not seem to fit with the character of God, but we grin and bear them and feel that we must faithfully plod on trying to discern his will for us. Trying to discover guidance like this reduces many disciples to feeling that they are spies, forced by one underhanded method or another to pry out precious information from a foreign power that seems reluctant to part with it. Is this what it is meant to be like? Perhaps not.

The problem is that many of us are too preoccupied with the idea of God's individual will for our lives and spend too long trying to fish out the plan he has filed away with our name on it somewhere in the offices of heaven. We must frankly face the fact that such a view of guidance throws up major difficulties for us in two areas. The first is biblical; the second is practical.

BIBLICAL DIFFICULTIES

The truth is that the Bible does not use the phrase "the will of God" in this connection nor does it show his people to be concerned with finding out what is on the map. It uses the term "will of God" only in the senses we have just explored of the sovereign or the moral will of God. But how do we square that assertion with the strong belief we began with that the Bible teaches that we can be sure that God will guide and direct our lives?

We believe that God guides us because he is the God of providence, and the doctrine of providence teaches that God is still intricately involved in the running of his universe. He did not create it in the distant past and then withdraw from it. In Calvin's words, "The providence we mean is not one by which the Deity, sitting idly by in heaven, looks on at what is taking place in the world, but one by which he, as it were, holds the helm and overrules all events." Those "events" include our lives. He holds the helm there, too, for he is not only the God who controls the solar system but the one who has numbered even the very hairs on our heads (Matthew 10:30). But that is different from the idea of God having an individual plan for us that we have to discover. We have so often wrongly translated the one idea into the other.

This doctrine of providence is crucial, running counter to some popular myths about God. *It contradicts deism*, the belief that although God made the world, he is now detached from it and uninvolved, like a washing machine manufacturer who, having made the machine, sells it to someone else and has nothing more to do with it. (God remains intimately involved.) *It contradicts fatalism*, which views God as impersonal and says what will be will be. (God is personally involved in a living and dynamic way.) *It contradicts the idea that chance is in control*, and asserts firmly that the living God is at the helm and remains in command.

PRACTICAL DIFFICULTIES

The second area of difficulty is practical. Garry Friesen, in a rigorous exposure of the idea of "finding the dot," as he calls it, or following the map, has listed a whole number of practical problems we run into when we base our search for guidance on this idea. They are readily recognizable. They are:

1. *It leads to indecision* and we waste time. We delay coming to a decision about which way to go, because we are fearful that we may get God's will for our lives wrong. We are so afraid of misreading the map that we do not move forward at all.

2. *It leads to compartmentalization*. We compartmentalize our lives into two types of decision. One compartment contains the minor decisions about which we do not seek guidance and the other compartment contains the major decisions about which we do. We sometimes have problems as to which decision belongs in which compartment.

3. *It leads to immaturity.* Rather than taking responsibility for our own lives, what we do, in effect, is abdicate that responsibility and leave it all up to God. That means that when things go wrong or we change our mind, we can blame God. "He told us to do it!"

4. *It leads to subjectivity.* In the end it boils down to the fact that no one can deny what we "feel led" to do, or argue about what we say God has told us to do, however foolish the idea might be. To say that God told us to do it is unanswerable.

5. *It leads to uncertainty.* It does not solve the problem of equal options. We speak of "going through the open door," but what happens when we are faced with two or more open doors? It helps us to decide which one we should go through.

As a pastor I have seen the outworking of just these problems in many people's lives, often with very detrimental effects not only on those seeking guidance but on their families, friends, and colleagues, too. There must be a better way.

So do we mean that God has no plan for our lives? Do we mean that life is a blank sheet of paper until we write on it the choices we make, with the possibility that we catch God unawares? Of course not! The sovereign Lord of the universe cannot be caught off-guard or unawares. Nothing you do is unknown to him before you do it. He knows the end from the beginning and reigns supreme over it all to bring about what he wants in your life. It simply means that you should not go about searching for guidance as if it were some secret plan that God is reluctant to let you see. We are called to other things.

Rejecting a rigid view of God's plan for our lives also helps us to recognize that there are many areas in which the Christian has freedom to choose what course of action he is to take. Unless something is mentioned specifically in God's moral law, either as something we should do or something we should not do, we may assume that the Christian is at liberty to act as he or she wishes in the matter.

This is the stand taken by Paul in Romans 14 when some Christians were keen to impose their particular viewpoint about special days and meat offered to idols on their fellow believers. Paul insists that there is no moral law involved and therefore they are free to do as they wish and have no right to judge others for the choices they make.

Of course, they were not free to act glibly or recklessly. There were principles of God's Word that applied to the way they made their choice and thus indirectly governed its outcome: They were to think carefully about the issue and not just rush in (verse 5); they were also to make sure they did not put any stumbling block in the way of another Christian's spiritual growth (verses 13 and 15); they were also to remember that they were accountable to God and had to do whatever they chose for him (verses 4, 9–11, and 18).

The same liberty is ours about all issues that the moral law of God does not cover. Thus, providing that always we remember the spirit in which decisions are to be made, we have freedom to come to our own decisions about what job we do, what course we study, whether we marry or stay single, what church we attend, and a great many other matters that are not mentioned in God's moral law.

The liberty that God has given us in these matters is an awesome responsibility. It is not surprising that many look for easier approaches and wish that God does have a plan in which he has already made all the decisions for us. But Scripture encourages us to approach the question of guidance differently, recognizing the liberty of choice that is ours.

In the rest of this book we shall look at how this all works out in practice—at how God does guide us in the choices we face through the decisions we make.☐

Chapter 4

Normal Guidance For Normal People

Christian biographies cause problems! I suppose you have to be somewhat exceptional to get your story into print and that explains why, taken as a whole, biographies seem to give a quite distorted impression about how God guides, as they do about many other features of the Christian life. Reading these books, one might get the idea that unless you have had a visit from an angel, a vision of the house you are to live in ten years hence, or received a word of prophecy, gift-wrapped and addressed with your name on it, there is something wrong with you.

Do not be misled! God can and does guide through angels, visions, prophecies, and other spectacular ways, too. We shall explore these means of guidance in the next chapter. They are not the usual means of guidance he uses for his people—for the most part, they are much more humdrum. Guidance is not by any means always sensationally communicated, spectacularly easy, nor unmistakably clear.

So what is God's normal way to guide normal people?

USE YOUR MIND

The basic principle in searching for guidance is that we need to use our minds! What a letdown! Is all we have to say about guidance only that when people are looking for it, they should think things through for themselves? If so, where does God come into play and how are we different from others who have no God to whom they look for direction? What about all the other means of guidance of which the Bible speaks? Is not such an emphasis on the mind purely Christian rationalism and a denial of the more supernatural dimension of Christian experience?

Unrepentantly I repeat that the first principle in seeking guidance is that Christians should use their minds, thinking through the choices they confront, and decisions they must make. Many Christians get into trouble precisely because they fail to grasp this and rely first and foremost on other means of guidance. The difference between us Christians and unbelievers is not *whether* we should use our minds but *how* we use them. Let me explain. There are three key issues we need to grasp.

THE PLACE OF PLANNING

Psalm 32:9 suggests that we are not animals who have to be controlled automatically by a superior power and who have no choice about where to turn. As people we

are different. We have choice and the capacity to come
to wise decisions if we care to use the faculties God
has given us. It is for this reason that the Bible
constantly emphasizes that we should take the initiative and the responsibility, and we should plan for the
future.

We sometimes think of planning as unspiritual
because it seems to confine God and restrict what he
might want us to do. It seems to take our lives out of
God's hands and put the control firmly within our
grasp. It is often said to be opposed to the spontaneity
that gives the Holy Spirit room to work.

Apparently, the Bible has no such inhibitions. It
sees planning not as in opposition to giving God
freedom to shape our future but as the usual, though
not infallible, way in which God may do precisely
that. It shows no embarrassment at all in instructing
the believer to engage in planning.

> The plans of the righteous are just,
> but the advice of the wicked is deceitful.
> > Proverbs 12:5

> Commit to the LORD whatever you do,
> and your plans will succeed.
> > Proverbs 16:3

> Make plans by seeking advice;
> if you wage war, obtain guidance.
> > Proverbs 20:18

> The plans of the diligent lead to profit
> as surely as haste leads to poverty.
> > Proverbs 21:5

A wise man has great power,
and a man of knowledge increases strength.

Proverbs 24:5

And with a simple homely illustration it instructs,

Finish your outdoor work
and get your fields ready;
after that, build your house.

Proverbs 24:27

Similarly, the New Testament shows no embarrassment about planning. Paul obviously saw the need for it in his ministry and never rejected it as unspiritual. He shows no preference for some notion that all he has to do is sit back and let God do the driving. What he objects to, as the Bible consistently does, is plans that are made "in a worldly manner" (2 Corinthians 1:17). When he wrote those words, he was thinking of the way in which we often make promises without thinking at all and just as quickly break them, to the cost of those to whom they were made. Such plans lack not only thought but integrity and respect. They are the sort of plans we make just to shut someone up but without having any real intention of keeping them. That is "worldly."

But the issue of worldliness is broader. James 4:13–17 speaks of people who make plans for tomorrow arrogantly. They do so without any reference to God, as if their lives were not at God's disposal. In reality, our knowledge of the future is extremely limited. We do not know what tomorrow holds. Such a thought ought to encourage us to be humble, since we should realize that if we cannot even predict the future with certainty how much less can we be confident about controlling it. This is the point that the book of Proverbs had earlier made abundantly clear in a number of verses that complement but do not contradict those that stress the need for planning. For example,

> To man belong the plans of the heart,
> but from the LORD comes the reply of the tongue.
> > Proverbs 16:1

> In the heart a man plans his course,
> but the LORD determines his steps.
> > Proverbs 16:9

> Many are the plans in a man's heart,
> but it is the LORD's purpose that prevails.
> > Proverbs 19:21

> Do not boast about tomorrow,
> for you do not know what a day may bring forth.
> > Proverbs 27:1

We should not interpret these verses as if they were telling us not to plan. Far from it. They are simply reminding us that the plans we make can only ever be partial and provisional. Even so, with humility and an openness to God to direct otherwise, let us move ahead to plan, to prepare wisely and thoughtfully for the future, and to take full responsibility for having done so.

John Calvin was far from being the stuffy theologian we often accuse him of being. In fact, he was a great pastor and he writes pertinently on this issue of planning. Using Solomon as an example, he shows how human planning is perfectly consistent with God's sovereignty.

> Regarding future events, Solomon easily reconciles human deliberation with divine providence, for while he derides the stupidity of those who presume to undertake anything without God, as if they were not ruled by his hand, he elsewhere thus expresses himself: "A man's heart deviseth his way, but the Lord directeth his steps," (Proverbs 16:9), intimating that the eternal decrees of God by no means prevent us from proceeding, under his will, to provide for ourselves, and arrange all our affairs. And the reason for this is clear. For he who has fixed the boundaries of our life, has at the same time entrusted us with the care of it, provided us with the means of preserving it, forewarned us of the dangers to which we are exposed, and supplied cautions and remedies that we may not be overwhelmed unawares. Now our duty is clear; namely, since the Lord has committed to us the defense of our life—to defend it; since he offers assistance—to use it; since he forewarns us of danger—not to rush on heedless; since he supplies remedies—not to neglect them. . . . God has been pleased to conceal from us all future events that we may prepare for them as doubtful, and cease not to apply the provided remedies until they have either been overcome, or have proved too much for our care. Hence, . . . the Providence of God does not interpose simply (operate directly); but, by employing means, assumes as it were, a visible form.
>
> (*Institutes of the Christian Religion,* I, 17:4)

So God intends us to use the means he has put at our disposal. God works through means. Among those means are the minds he has given us that we should use to inquire, to weigh carefully the merits of options before us, then to choose, taking full responsibility for the decision once we have made it. In other words, God expects us to plan.

THE PLACE OF RENEWAL

If the basic principle of guidance is that we should use our own minds to determine our answers, two questions come to mind. The first is, can we trust our minds? Are we not full of hidden motives and disguised desires that will lead us astray? Do we not have to admit that our knowledge is very limited and our understanding corrupt? The second question is, in what way does this make the Christian different from the non-Christian?

Both of these questions find an answer in the New Testament's teaching about the renewal of the mind, which is part and parcel of our salvation.

The unbeliever, according to Paul, is futile in his thinking, darkened in his understanding, and ignorant (Ephesians 4:17–18). Humanity's original rebellion against God (Genesis 3:1–24) had a major effect on the ability of men and women to think. Since that point in time, people have been unable to think straight or to be unerringly truthful in their minds. "Desire" has ruled over us, just as God predicted it would. So our perceptions are all askew and our understanding is warped and out of alignment with God.

This is what the theologians call "total depravity." The doctrine does not mean that everything we do is evil and that we are incapable of doing any good. Plainly, there are many good people around and there is a great deal of good that people do. It means, rather, that everything we do is infected by minds that are less than pure; even our thinking is corrupt.

When a person becomes a believer, that changes. Part of the wonder of our multifaceted salvation is that we are "made new in the attitudes of your minds" (Ephesians 4:23). The Holy Spirit gives us a new disposition. "The interior principle that really governs and controls and operates the mind itself," to quote Dr. Martyn Lloyd-Jones, is renewed. We have a new ability to think differently; to think in new ways; to see things from God's perspective; to be concerned to glorify him; to distinguish between right and wrong and to be concerned to do right; to discriminate between what is a worthy and an unworthy ambition. The new spirit in our minds should captivate and control us.

There is plenty of evidence that this happens. Many young converts become worried shortly after conversion because they feel more guilty and troubled about sin than ever before. This is the renewed mind at work, causing them to have new standards more akin to God's than once they had. Then there is often a new appreciation of the Bible and a hunger to read God's Word. Time and again in very practical ways I have seen this renewed mind at work in those recently converted. One person was engaged in wrong sexual relations when converted. No one, except the Holy

Spirit, taught him that they were wrong and had to end. But he ended them immediately. Another owned a video shop and, once converted, immediately destroyed his dirty videos and cleaned up his business. Incidentally, he was engaged in doing so when a local newspaper reporter entered his shop and asked him what he was doing, with the result that it made front page news in the local press. These are examples of the renewed mind at work.

So the orientation of the believer's mind is different. The driving power has changed. In Dr. Martyn Lloyd-Jones's words, "If the spirit of our mind is changed and is renewed, we shall be thinking in such a way that we shall put off the old man and will put on the new man."

This helps us to understand that attractive, but often misapplied verse, in Psalm 37:4, which reads, "Delight yourself in the LORD and he will give you the desires of your heart." How many a young Christian has dreamed that if only he behaved himself as a Christian, God would give him that new guitar, motorbike, or car ... or even girl, which was the "desire of his heart." But that is not what it means at all. The secret to it lies in the opening words, "Delight yourself in the LORD." If you are doing that, God will form in you new desires and ambitions for himself and his work, which will replace less worthy ambitions. A new agenda will be set. Desires for things like cars or other material possessions will go out of the window, though not necessarily the ability to appreciate them. Here is an example of the renewed mind at work.

But we must not suppose that this occurs without

a daily commitment to it on our part. Remember that we are not computers. God has not taken out one chip and simply programmed us with another. The teaching of Ephesians 4:22 is that we have had our minds renewed so that we are able to put off the old nature and put on the new—but we must do the putting off and putting on.

Romans 12:2 shows that this has a direct connection with questions of guidance. It summarizes as follows: "Do not conform any longer to the pattern of this world, but be transformed by the renewing of your mind. Then you will be able to test and approve what God's will is—his good, pleasing and perfect will."

Thus, the mind of the Christian is different from the mind of the unbeliever because the operation of the Holy Spirit has transformed it. And, with daily consecration to God, the Christian is able by using this renewed mind to discern God's will for him. The renewed mind, therefore, has a vital place in the way in which we are guided.

This explains why Paul, as we have seen, when writing to the Romans about issues of dispute among them, does not settle the issue by making an *ex cathedra* statement that imposes some new law on them. He informs them that it is quite legitimate for Christians to take different stands on meat offered to idols, or on the value of special days, as long as a major guiding principle in coming to a decision about the matter in addition to the other things mentioned (page 53), is that "each one should be fully convinced in his own mind" (Romans 14:5) about the stand he takes.

A convinced mind is a major factor in guidance.

We may legitimately believe we are guided when we feel a conviction that a certain course of action or decision is right. This is different from the shallow inner feelings of peace mentioned somewhat skeptically before. This is no self-gratifying emotion. Conviction arises after thought and prayer and in the full consciousness of our responsibilities to others and to God. If our convictions stand the test these may bring, then we may justly feel it is God guiding us. As we examine the call of the prophets or the decisions of the apostles, we cannot escape the fact that in the end so often they acted on the basis of conviction.

There are still numerous issues on which Christians conscientiously differ and where Christians legitimately have freedom to choose what to do. The answer to such untidiness is not to impose a new set of rules on it to flatten it into a dull uniformity. It was from such legalism that Christ came to set us free (Galatians 5:1). The answer is for Christians to use their own minds to think through their position, conscientiously, prayerfully, and considerately with minds that are informed by biblical teaching. If they do, they will be exercising the renewed mind that they have through the Holy Spirit.

THE PLACE OF WISDOM

Given that there is a need for planning and that we have the ability to plan in a way that is pleasing to God because our minds have been renewed by the Spirit, how in practice are we to come to decisions?

The key to this question lies, as many have suggested with good reason, in the idea of "wisdom."

Wisdom is a notion we associate with the Old Testament, but it is not just an idea we encounter there. It is one we meet in the New Testament as well. Ephesians 5:15–16 instructs Christians to "be very careful, then, how you live—not as unwise but as wise, making the most of every opportunity, because the days are evil." Similarly, Colossians 4:5 says, "Be wise in the way you act toward outsiders; make the most of every opportunity."

Paul frequently talks about wisdom. According to Acts 15:38, it was the way he came to some major decisions about his own missionary strategy. According to Colossians 1:28, it was the way in which he set about teaching people to grow to maturity in Christ. According to Romans 16:19, his desire for his fellow Christians was that they should be "wise about what is good, and innocent about what is evil." High on his prayer agenda for his new converts was that they would receive wisdom (Ephesians 1:17; Colossians 1:9). And in Colossians 3:16 he instructs Christians to "teach and admonish one another with all wisdom."

In a celebrated verse that we often mention in prayer when we are seeking guidance, James also mentions the importance of wisdom. He wrote, "If any of you lacks wisdom, he should ask God, who gives generously to all without finding fault, and it will be given to him" (1:5). Having prayed for it, we often then forget that God, according to James, will generously give us what we asked for, and we flap around still looking for answers as if God has failed to do so.

So what is that "wisdom" that is to be the basis on which decisions are to be made? It is simply the ability to discern what is going to be spiritually right and beneficial in the choices we face. Garry Friesen describes it as "the ability to figure out what is spiritually expedient in a given situation."

James Packer speaks of it as "the power to see and the inclination to choose the best and the highest good." A seasoned Bible commentator, J. Armitage Robinson, said that wisdom was "the knowledge which sees into the heart of things, which knows them as they really are."

Once we see that God wishes us to come to decisions by using wisdom as a judge, we shall be freed from the fear often involved in trying to find out God's individual will or map for our lives. We can see that we might confront a number of perfectly reasonable choices; for instance, about a future job or even a future husband. It may be quite all right before God either to work for firm X or firm Y, either to marry A or B. There may not be just one right choice. Our responsibility is to choose wisely. Then we can have a clear conscience before God.

If we operate on this basis, we will find that it answers a host of questions. It gives us some perspective as we weigh the conflicting elements of the prospects before us and try to come to a decision about them.

We may face the opportunity of promotion, but is it wise to accept it? Wisdom will show us whether it is spiritually expedient if it gives us more influence for the cause of the kingdom of God or perhaps more money to give to God's work, assuming that we are spiritually mature enough for God to trust us with either of these increased responsibilities. It will be spiritually inexpedient if it will cause great strain in our family because it will turn us into workaholics, or if it leads us away from work for Christ, or separates us from the fellowship of God's people.

The way of wisdom will cause one person to accept in one set of circumstances, given his or her particular gifts or personality, while another will reject because his or her circumstances are different or they are not so strong spiritually and would not survive the additional responsibilities.

Wisdom always keeps before us what is *spiritually* best. We so often decide on the basis of what is *materially* best. This has resulted in many becoming less zealous for God and even less contented in themselves. Material riches do not necessarily make for happiness. They only do so if God intends that we have them and can be trusted to be good stewards of them.

The perspective of wisdom can be applied universally. Should you marry Jane or not? Well, is it wise to do so? Will the things the Bible teaches about marriage, including the way in which partners ought to stimulate one another to grow spiritually, be found in your marriage to Jane or not? Do you share much in common with Jane? Will she be possessive of you to the extent that she will come between you and your work within the church, or will she share that work with you? Does her attitude toward money cause concern? Does she appear to have a different agenda as far as material ambitions are concerned than you do? She's vivacious and full of fun, but is she aware of the effect she has on other men? If there are plenty of positive things in your relationship and no major stumbling blocks, then why not marry her? It could be that if you wait, there would be some other young woman who would fit the same picture and you are scared about missing "Miss Right." But where in the Bible are we taught that there is a "Miss Right" for us all? Rather, there may be several who might well be suitable, and we are free within that group to decide as wisdom directs.

The perspective of wisdom may equally be applied to the question of whether you remain single and do not get married at all. Circumstances may remove the choice in the matter for some but not by any means for all. Wisdom may decide the issue and lead some to choose to remain single. Perhaps the chosen career or vocation involves particular pressures, such as extensive travel or study, which would mean that any spouse, let alone any children, would be neglected. Perhaps one's personality lends itself to the single state because freedom and independence are highly valued, or fear of commitment and intimacy makes marriage too difficult to face. Singleness, even without these plain pointers, may be a positive choice before God, and wisdom will encourage some to choose it.

Similarly, the perspective of wisdom can be applied to seeking entrance to a Bible college. We may look forward to studies we can do there—they may lead us to a spiritual high. But is it wise? Wisdom will mean that we make sure that we have a clear call from God and have a goal so that the huge investment we are making in training is not going to be wasted on an ego trip or a spiritual holiday. Wisdom will ask us to face up to other responsibilities we have and not to indulge our own spiritual appetites selfishly. We will have to ask, Does the church feel I am gifted to go in this direction? Am I able to cope financially? And what will a prolonged course of study do to my marriage or family? Wisdom may well say to some, "Go ahead," while to others wisdom might suggest they should not pursue it.

A COMMENTARY ON WISDOM

The greatest commentary on wisdom is obviously to be found in the book of Proverbs. The way to be wise is to fear the Lord (1:7, 3:7, 9:10, and 15:33) and it assures us that "the fear of the LORD is a fountain of life" (14:27). We should be anxious, therefore, to know what it teaches, for there are many Christians whose lives do not seem to be lively fountains. Rather than running freely, being full of life and spontaneity, having a deep reservoir from which to draw when they face trouble, and having a refreshing feel to them—all characteristics of a good fountain—the lives of many Christians seem to be a damp trickle or even to be running dry, and never more so than when they are struggling with the question of guidance.

So what does it mean to "fear the Lord"? Proverbs answers that question in very practical and down-to-earth terms. That has caused many Christians to look at it and dismiss it in preference for bits of the Bible they consider more spiritual. Its spirituality is certainly different from that which you find elsewhere, but that does not make it less worthy.

The book of Proverbs advocates careful planning; investing time in preparation before expecting responsibility or rewards; the value of hard work; efficient time-keeping; the need to seek the opinions of others; weighing carefully the consequences of our proposed actions; thinking before jumping; looking before leaping; knowing your place; the significance of handling social relationships properly; the need for teachableness and humility, and the importance of avoiding temptation and folly.

It would seem that finding guidance, from the perspective of the book of Proverbs, is about making wise decisions. That is the secret. When we do so, we can be sure that God has guided.

The apostles found their guidance in this way, more often than not. We shall look in the next chapter at other ways in which God guided them, but for now, note carefully what the New Testament actually says about the decisions they made. In handling the dispute that arose because Greek-speaking widows were being overlooked in the church's sharing of the resources, the apostles settled the matter by saying, "It would not be right for us . . . " (Acts 6:2). At the Council of Jerusalem where they needed the guidance of God, if ever they needed it, we keep reading of the way they "decided to choose" or "agreed to choose" or just that "it seemed good to the Holy Spirit and to us . . . " (Acts 15:22, 25, and 28).

Paul writes in similar terms about decisions. He says about his own arrangements: "We thought it best" (1 Thessalonians 3:1), or "if it seems advisable for me to go" (1 Corinthians 16:4). Or to the Philippians he writes, "I think it is necessary to send back to you Epaphroditus" (2:25).

Far from sitting around seeking guidance and expecting bolts from the blue, the apostles seem to have gone about their business, making wise decisions and believing that in doing so God was guiding them.

CONCLUSION

Normal guidance, then, involves making decisions for ourselves wisely, with humility and prayer, so that we might be open to God. It involves planning and using minds that God has not only given to us as his creatures but renewed for us in Christ through the Holy Spirit. Too often we look for more direct methods of guidance because it lets us off the hook of doing the hard thinking and taking the responsibility for the decisions we have reached. But Christ calls us to maturity and in this area, as in others, we need to measure up to "the whole measure of the fullness of Christ" (Ephesians 4:13). He came not to make us less human and less responsible but more human and more responsible.

After speaking on this subject on one occasion, I was handed the following poem. I have never been able to track down the source, but I am grateful to the

one who gave it to me since it sums up the principles
we have set out.

Lord, the trouble is
I want it all cut and dried,
a clear path set out for me,
an easy set of instructions,
a route map I can't possibly misinterpret.
And what would I call it?
The lazy man's guide to the kingdom?
And you the courier,
helping with the luggage,
moving me smoothly from one hotel to the
    next,
taking care of all the problems,
life, one long holiday.

You expect more of me than that, Lord.
You show me the real world of choices,
questions I have to face, decisions to make,
tensions I must learn to balance
as I move along the road.
I need the quiet times with you,
the times when we can sort out the
    relationship,
just you and me,
when we can concentrate on who and what I
    am.
But who and what I am only become real
back in the world outside.
You were the Christ throughout your life
but without the focus of the cross
your purpose would be blurred, half done,

and that's not done at all.

But doing needs a center point
to give stability and strength,
a starting place, from which the purpose comes.
So one's no use without the other.
The building needs foundations
and I begin to see my hopes for what they are:
Child's dreams of life, clear cut
though not so innocent and feather cushioned
    from reality,
served up, well cooked on a warm plate.

Life's tougher than that,
the choices must be made
and with each choice
the risk of right or wrong.
The tensions stay, but so do you
to share it with me.

I am content.
No, that's not true,
I'm not.
But I'll settle for the uncertainty
with you. □

Chapter 5

Bolts from the Blue

Like it or not, we seem to think that guidance was different for the early church. As we read our New Testaments, it looks to us as if they were always receiving "bolts from the blue" that told them clearly which way they were to go. Even if we accept that they came to much of their guidance by making wise decisions in the way set out in the previous chapter, is it not still true that they experienced a number of supernatural forms of guidance? What were they and what significance do they have for us?

God is not limited in the way in which he chooses to guide us. He does not have to guide us exclusively through our making wise decisions. As the living God he can, if he so chooses, intervene directly and give us direction ... and he does. But before rushing headlong to see how we can increase this sort of divine intervention in our lives, let us investigate the facts. What supernatural means of guidance did they receive in the New Testament?

SUPERNATURAL MEANS OF GUIDANCE

Dreams

In the Old Testament, dreams seem to have been a method God frequently used to show his people the way forward. Joseph not only foresaw his own life through dreams (Genesis 37:2–11) but was much involved in unraveling the mystery of other people's dreams and telling them what futures they held for them (Genesis 40 and 41). Gideon found direction and encouragement from a dream (Judges 7:13–15). Solomon encountered God in a dream at a decisive point at the beginning of his reign (1 Kings 3:5). And, of course, Daniel was much taken up with interpreting the dreams of his own and his rulers (Daniel 2, 4, and 7) through which he made known the future.

In the New Testament, Joseph, the husband of Mary, and the Magi were spoken to through dreams and in that way received their unexpected travel instructions, causing them to be safe from Herod's evil plans (Matthew 2:12–14). It is surprising, though, that there is only one other dream recorded in the New Testament—the dream that Pilate's wife experienced that resulted in her warning her husband not to have anything to do with the unjust trial of Jesus (Matthew 27:19). It was advice that he ignored.

None of the apostles seems to have been guided by dreams, and there is little encouragement elsewhere in the New Testament to think that this may be a frequent channel that God now uses to offer guidance.

Some, however, feel themselves to be guided by

dreams and argue that there is more support in the Bible for doing so than I have yet admitted. They speak of the way in which it was accepted that prophets would receive the word of the Lord through a dream. Once or twice the Old Testament suggests that this was a well-known method by which they derived their messages (Numbers 12:6; Jeremiah 23:25–28). They also point out that dreaming dreams was said to be a mark of the work of the Holy Spirit, which from Pentecost onward we could confidently expect to happen as a matter of course to the elderly in the church (Acts 2:17).

All that is true, but care must be taken with these references. In fact, Jeremiah, in the verses referred to, castigates prophets who claim to have found the word of the Lord in a dream and dismisses their dreams as "delusions of their own minds." On other occasions he is equally dismissive of great store being put on dreams and rebukes the children of Israel for encouraging dreamers (Jeremiah 29:8). The prophet Ezekiel adopts a similarly scornful attitude toward those who have false visions (Ezekiel 13).

As for Joel's prophecy, quoted on the Day of Pentecost, it seems more of a general reference to the people of God as a whole now having become a visionary people rather than a reference to obtaining specific guidance through dreams.

The true picture is that as with Moses, so with the people of the New Covenant. God spoke with him "face to face, clearly and not in riddles" (Numbers 12:8). The expectation of the new covenant was that this would be how God would instruct all his people

(Jeremiah 31:33–34). God's communication with his people through his Spirit is no longer expected to be an enigmatic riddle.

Dreams have always been open to numerous interpretations and our understanding of them has been greatly complicated since the advent of psychology. One does not have to agree with Freud's novel speculations about their significance to realize that they are some form of release for a jumble of motives, experiences, fears, desires, and subconscious feelings that are deep within us. Because they reveal something of our true identity and deeply hidden psyche, they are of much value to counselors and spiritual directors. From dreams counselors are able to understand more about the people they help and to use them both to help people come to understand themselves and as a basis for giving wise spiritual direction.

Not all dreams have the same significance. Possibly their greatest value in searching for guidance is an indirect one—that is, in telling us things about ourselves that might otherwise lie hidden from us and so provide us with material to inform our wise decision making. But some might come with great clarity and remain with us with great conviction in our wakened state. It would seem that these are messengers of God we must act upon.

My pastoral experience would, however, lead me to suggest we should be very careful in relying on dreams. Far from giving any certain guidance, my experience of talking to those who feel guided in this way suggests that they may sometimes be clutching at dreams as drowning men clutch at straws. They want to be guided to do this or that and the dream seems in some mysterious and partial way to confirm it. That is hardly surprising if dreams are really revealing the hidden us. Too often the reality we have to face when awake is different.

Visions

Visions differ from dreams in that they are sense impressions we receive while awake. In contrast to dreams, these seem to have been an accepted occurrence for the apostles. Saul saw a vision of the exalted Christ on the Damascus Road, and Ananias likewise received a vision from God on the basis of which he went to minister to the blinded Saul (Acts 9:10–16). Given the fearsome reputation Saul had gained as a persecutor of the church, it would probably have taken nothing less than a vision to persuade Ananias to go anywhere near Saul.

Peter, similarly, had a vision one day when he was on a rooftop in Joppa, praying before lunch. It was this vision that persuaded him to overcome a lifetime of prejudice and go to preach the gospel to a Gentile soldier called Cornelius. Peter's vision coincided with one that Cornelius himself had, as a result of which he sent for Peter to come and preach to him (Acts 10).

At specific turning points in Paul's missionary career we read that he received a vision. It happened in Troas when he was uncertain about which way to go next (Acts 16:9–10), and it kept him in Corinth when he might have wished to run away (Acts 18:9). On other occasions, too, he had visions (Acts 22:17–21;

2 Corinthians 12:1). Likewise, the book of Revelation was a vision given to John about the church when it was under threat of annihilation.

The impressive thing about many of these visions is that they have to do with mission. They occur at times when there are significant new initiatives in evangelism: the conversion of a future missionary to the Gentiles; evangelism to the pagan Gentiles; a breakthrough into Macedonia; a refusal to give up in Corinth, or the onslaught of such a violent persecution that the very existence of the church is threatened. Without them the vital steps may well not have been taken, or the power to endure might have been lacking.

The other visions Paul speaks of having (2 Corinthians 12:1–6) do not really help us to understand much more about visions, since he says the content of them was inexpressible and, in any case, he is not permitted to reveal it. The primary value of these visions might well lie in their strengthening of the personal relationship between Paul and his Lord. Even so, they would seem to fit the general picture, for he speaks about being "caught up to the third heaven." It would appear that visions consistently reveal God's perspective on current issues or on specific situations being faced by the church. They are not simply the thoughts of "visionary leaders" but a peep behind the scenes of heaven.

Perhaps that gives us a clue as to how we should assess visions we or others might have. Are they really providing significant guidance about the advance of the church into new territory, or causing God's

83

servants to "stick in there" where the territory seems tough? In what way do they encourage us by unmasking our earthly situation, or by challenging our human feelings and show us eternal realities and God's perspectives?

Angels

On a few occasions God sent heavenly messengers to give direction to his servants. An angel came to Philip to direct him to leave his successful evangelistic campaign in Samaria and go and witness to one man in the desert (Acts 8:26). Peter was prompted by an angel to escape from prison, not once but twice (Acts 5:19; 12:7−8). In the middle of a shipwreck, Paul was fortified by an angel and told what his future destiny was to be so that he himself could be encouraged and encourage others that the disaster they were experiencing was not going to be fatal (Acts 27:23).

The New Testament does not mention angels simply as agents of guidance. It even hints at the existence of personal guardian angels (Matthew 18:10 and Acts 12:15), usually, one assumes, in an invisible guise. In view of this and their earlier well developed role as messengers of God, it is perhaps surprising that we do not see them more frequently providing the early Christians with guidance.

What strikes me about the occasions when they do give the Lord's servants clear directions rather than provide behind-the-scenes protection, is that on each occasion the circumstances are extreme. Probably most evangelists would need an angel to convince them of the absurdity of leaving a successful mass crusade for Christ in Samaria to witness to one man in a desert. Similarly, escaping James-Bond-style from prisons and shipwrecks is not a run-of-the-mill experience, even for apostles.

I know of only one person who claims to have been guided by an angel and I do not doubt his story. A visitor to Eastern Europe was forced to arrive in a town where he hoped to meet a Christian leader at dusk one night without any address or directions as to where the Christian leader could be found. He tells me that a man appeared from nowhere, silently beckoned him, and led him to his precise destination, then disappeared just as mysteriously as he had arrived. Whether the stranger was a human or not, my friend could not tell. But he knew that the stranger was a messenger from God. In such extreme situations it seems entirely realistic that God should still offer guidance through angels.

An Audible Voice

"God spoke to me and told me to do it," we say. Philosophers have spent ages poring over the meaning of those words. "What do we mean?" they ask. "Do we mean we actually heard his voice in the same audible manner as we hear a human voice?" For the most part, we confess that when God speaks to us it is not quite like that; it is just that his will seems so clear in the impression it makes on us that it is *as if* he spoke to us.

Some want to testify that they have actually and audibly heard the voice of God as they would hear a human voice. I have met one or two people like this whose holiness of character makes me believe that they are right. Some who have received such a privileged form of guidance are well-known Christian leaders. Some are quite ordinary. I think of one who actually became a Christian not only because the Lord spoke to her in this way but because he actually laughed at her, too. It happened in the early hours of the morning while she was alone doing night duty in her hospital. Fortunately, it did not result in the patients' being awakened.

Thus, God can and does still speak as he used to. According to Acts he spoke to Philip like this (8:29), to Paul (9:3–6; 23:11) and to Peter (10:19–20).

We should note that such conversations are not recorded as everyday affairs. They were reserved for occasions when God had something really special to say, such as when Jesus was baptized, or transfigured before his inner band of disciples. On both occasions God spoke with an audible voice to authenticate that Jesus was his Son and that people should pay the closest attention to what he had to say.

If we believe that God has spoken to us in such a manner, the best advice is to do what he has said. The outcome will eventually prove whether we were right to believe it was the voice of God or whether, for some reason or another, we were mistaken.

Physical Miracles

Among the many miracles in the Acts, one has special relevance to the question of guidance. It left the person involved no choice about the direction he was to take. In Acts 8:39–40 we read, "The Spirit of the Lord suddenly took Philip away . . . Philip, however, appeared at Azotus and traveled about, preaching the gospel in all the towns until he reached Caesarea." That certainly does not sound as though Philip made a normal departure from the situation!

If it made guidance a very simple matter for Philip, it must be said that miracles do not always guide with such startling clarity. Miracles need to be interpreted with the eyes of faith. Many people saw Jesus work miracles, but only a few came to believe in him as a result. Others dismissed him as a magician, or worse. It took faith to see the hand of God in his work. In our more secular age, people can still easily dismiss miracles as mere coincidences, the power of suggestion, hoaxes, or just plain luck. Jesus once remarked that not even a staggeringly sensational miracle would succeed in convincing some people of the need to prepare to meet their God (Luke 16:31). His words remain true. Faith is needed to discern God at work in such acts of power or signs and wonders.

It would be good if we could say that there were no Christian unbelievers, but regrettably, there are. Many Christians pray for guidance through a miracle, even if only a minor miracle! Yet, when God grants them their request, they often still doubt and question. Prayers are answered; help comes to hand;

situations change remarkably; resources are unexpectedly provided; healings take place, and Christians often still remain hesitant about believing the Lord, trusting his promise, or obeying his command for them. They lack the eyes of faith to see that it is God powerfully at work and speaking personally to them through the miraculous. They seem to have adopted the assumptions of the secularists.

Miracles themselves do not blind us into doing God's will. They require us to see them for what they are—a gracious act of God's power—and then they require us to freely submit ourselves to the consequences in our lives, whatever they may be. Think of the times when you have said, "If God does such and such, then I will do this for him." Or, "If God unexpectedly provides X amount of money, I will embark on this project for him even if I do not know where the rest of the money is going to come from." Or, "If God intervenes in my life by remarkably altering my circumstances, then I will obey him in this way." Have we always followed through on our commitments or have we sometimes explained away the miracle?

Prophecy

With prophecy we enter a vast, complex subject. Those who wish to explore its depth and breadth should look at one of the many books specifically devoted to it in recent days, especially *The Gift of Prophecy* by Wayne Grudem (Kingsway). Our interest is specific and our comments limited.

Prophecy has a long and varied history starting, of course, in the Old Testament. There the prophets revealed the moral will of God by reminding the children of Israel of the terms of their covenant with him and then astutely applying it all in such a way as to give specific direction to political and economic questions their leaders and contemporaries were facing. By the very nature of the case they often seemed to stand in opposition to their fellow Israelites.

In the New Testament the role of the prophet is somewhat different. No longer do they stand in opposition to the people of God but are to be found in a fully supportive role among them, and firmly within the church. No longer do they seem concerned about grand social and political issues but more about the affairs of the church. Their role is the "strengthening, encouragement and comfort" of their fellow believers (1 Corinthians 14:3).

The gift of prophecy often seems to be used most profitably today when it is in line with those purposes. It frequently comes to a church as a word of confirmation about decisions that are almost reached or have just been reached. It sometimes comes as an encouraging word of correction and an exhortation to greater things. Of course, it might come as a word or rebuke, like the letters to the seven churches in Revelation 2 and 3, but the dominant note in the New Testament teaching about the gift is on its positive and encouraging, not negative and condemning, role.

With that background and the assumption that we may define prophecy in some such terms as, "a message from the Lord borne in upon the messenger by the Spirit of God about a particular situation," in what way do we find the apostles or others being guided by prophecies in the early church? To judge by its popularity today, one would expect prophecy to be a frequent means of providing directions both for individuals and for churches. Although it is evident that the exercise of the gift of prophecy was common in the early church, as references to it in Acts 21:9 and 1 Corinthians 14 testify, we only have one concrete illustration of the way that it offered guidance to someone. It may be that prophecy was used to set apart Barnabas and Saul for missionary work in Acts 13:2, but it is not explicitly stated. The clear example is to be found in Acts 21:10–11.

Here, Agabus prophesies what Paul will encounter when he visits Jerusalem: "The Holy Spirit says, 'In this way the Jews of Jerusalem will bind the owner of this belt (i.e., Paul) and will hand him over to the Gentiles.'"

Just what did that prophecy mean and what intention did God have in voicing it through Agabus? The natural reaction of Paul's companions was to see it as a warning, and they tried to persuade Paul to change his plans and not go to Jerusalem. Paul did not understand it in these terms but took it rather as an added incentive to make the journey. He perceived that if he were indeed to be persecuted in Jerusalem, it would simply be a point of identification with Jesus his Lord, who had himself been persecuted in that city. How could he but go to Jerusalem? To him, the prophecy was a test of his commitment and a stimulus to his discipleship.

The Bible seems to me entirely realistic, as it always is, in leaving this as something of a puzzle. Prophecies that I have heard and received have not usually settled the matter. Rather, they have been an "encouraging" word from the Lord but a word that has still left me with the need to decide what I am going to do as a result of the words received.

ASSESSING SUPERNATURAL MEANS OF GUIDANCE

I firmly believe that God still guides through "bolts from the blue." Although these supernatural means of guidance may not be his normal method of guidance, he still uses them and they still have a place in Christian experience. Four situations in which these signs might come into play would seem more common than others.

First, God is a gracious God and is fully understanding of our human limitations. There are times, therefore, when even though he has given us direction through normal means, we may still be floundering and he steps in to speak in more impressive ways to move us along. Second, there are occasions when all the normal signals we might receive are missing, such as when we are in a foreign culture and do not know the language or have proper contacts or guides. Then, in his grace, he provides us with these comforting means of direction. Third, on other occasions the step we are required to take is so momentous that we are fearful and need the incentive of a more-than-usual means of guidance to give us courage. Fourth, there are yet further occasions when God may want us to do the unusual or unexpected and it would be easy for us to read the normal signals wrongly. He therefore interrupts the normal processes to make us think again.

Having said all that, these occasions are perhaps not such an advantage as we might at first consider them to be. They will not necessarily solve all our problems about guidance. Four cautionary remarks need to be made in the light of what we have learned so far.

They Are Not Unambiguous

Dreams, visions, prophecies all need interpreting. They are not usually so plain as to leave us no option but to behave in a certain way. The classic illustration of this is the one of Paul and Agabus. When Paul received the warning from Agabus, it did not stop him from going to Jerusalem. Was he right to do so, or should he have understood this prophecy as a "no entry" sign?

Most dreams, visions, and prophecies, not to mention the other methods of supernatural guidance, need interpreting. I think of a young man who came to see me once at college because he felt he had had a vision calling him into the ministry. At dusk one evening, he had, he said, been cleaning the candlesticks in the church where he was a server, when he looked up and saw a multitude of feet dancing in the rafters of the roof. He immediately recognized the feet as the feet of angels who were rejoicing that he was going to be a preacher of the gospel. That, he said, constituted his call.

I am glad the interpretation of that vision was so clear to him, but I confess it was not so clear to me. What I was hearing was his interpretation of what he had seen—an interpretation rendered doubtful by the complete lack of any supporting evidence that he had the gifts required to train as a full-time Christian worker. He certainly was not ready for training yet, and I was doubtful that he ever would be.

Moses, as we have seen, was distinguished from other servants of God in the Old Testament because God spoke to him plainly and not in riddles, as he did to others (Numbers 12:8). In the New Testament dispensation, it is how we can expect him, through the Holy Spirit, to speak to every believer.

They Are Not Infallible

Second, we need to be cautious of obtaining guidance through "bolts from the blue" because such bolts are not infallible! The idea is a minefield where we need to walk carefully, distinguishing between our imagination and God's revelation, and that is not always easy.

The growing recognition of the place of prophecy as a gift of the Spirit, which has a constructive and beneficial role to play within the church, is one I welcome and that, thankfully, I can testify has been used to beneficial effect in the lives of many believers. Yet, I have also seen it used falsely to damage believers and throw them off course. With hindsight, honesty compels us to admit that on such occasions the one prophesying is often expressing his or her own deeply felt longings rather than any word really received from the Lord.

Even some of the greatest of God's servants have fallen into such a trap. I was interested to read this about George Whitefield, whose experience has a familiar and contemporary ring about it.

> Prior to the birth of Whitefield's only child in October 1743, he declared his belief that the child would be a son and a preacher of the gospel. Four months later the infant who, as Whitefield "fondly hoped," "was to be great in the eyes of the Lord," died, and Whitefield at once recognized his mistaken expectation, saying, "I misapplied several texts of Scripture. Upon these grounds I made no scruple of declaring 'that I should have a son, and that his name should be John.'"

As Ian Murray, from whose biography on Jonathan Edwards this confession is taken, comments, "Many good souls, both among clergy and laity, for a while, mistook fancy for faith and imagination for revelation."

It still happens. I have heard prophecies about the sex of an expected baby, which have proved false, and I have heard prophecies predicting when childless couples would receive the gift of children from the Lord, which have been equally wrong. Sadly, those who have uttered such prophecies have rarely had the courage readily to admit their mistake as Whitefield did. They have usually conveniently forgotten their loud prophetic claims when events have proved false, or they have wriggled and squirmed in trying to spiritualize the plain facts away.

Remember, guidance through these supernatural means is not infallible any more than any other form of guidance is.

They Are Not Common

Without doubt God uses these means to offer guidance. We have seen the evidence for this from the New Testament. And yet, standing back from the specific evidence and gaining something of a broader perspective, we might be surprised at how little guidance was given through these means as distinct from more mundane means.

Once we leave the story of the early church as recorded in Acts, there are no concrete allusions in the rest of the New Testament to these "bolts from the blue" as means by which people in the church expected to be guided. First Corinthians 12 and 14 might well be alluding to such things in their discussion of the place of spiritual gifts in the church. Other than that, we are never told that people were guided this way, or that they should seek guidance this way. The emphasis, as we pointed out in the previous chapter, is much more on coming to prayerful and wise decisions.

They Are Not Superior

Scripture gives no indication that such supernatural means of guidance are superior to more natural means.

Some Christians give the impression that they believe in an athletic league table of guidance. Many Christians, they imply, are in division four and have no option but to score guidance goals by the rather sluggish and uninspired means of using their minds. Others, however, are in division one and they play on a different level. They score guidance goals by more exciting and supernatural means, the like of which we have been discussing.

It is a nice thought, but there is no foundation for it in the Bible. These methods of guidance are not superior, just different. They are not the means you graduate to after proving your abilities lower down in the league. They are the means God sometimes uses but more often does not, whoever you are.

So the upshot is this: God can and does guide through "bolts from the blue," but far from being a simpler or more privileged form of guidance, these means are fraught with as many problems as others. We may think that such means in which God seems to take more of an initiative in making a revelation known would be safer and clearer, but closer examination shows that this is not so. Perhaps God sometimes has to resort to such methods because our circumstances make it difficult to obtain guidance in other ways, or we are too stubborn to listen to anything else. When God does guide in such ways, we should rejoice . . . and still use our God-given faculty of discernment. We cannot do without it. If he does not, then we should not be downhearted. It does not mean he loves us any less.

Chapter 6

What About the Fleece?

On Friday December twentieth, Adrian Plass wrote in his diary:

> Laid a "fleece." If a midget in a Japanese admiral's uniform came to the door at 9:04 precisely, I would know that God wanted me to sing carols.
>
> 9:05: A miracle! No-one came. That's that then. Leonard Thynn came at 10:30 selling charity cards. Bought 50.*

WHAT IS "PUTTING OUT A FLEECE"?

It sounds vaguely old-fashioned to talk about "putting out fleeces." What on earth does it mean? The words may be old-fashioned, but the idea is certainly still very common. To lay a fleece is to propose to God that he gives you a certain sign on the basis of which you will take a certain course of action.

*The Sacred Diary of Adrian Plass, (Aged 37 3/4).

The person who originally "laid a fleece" was Gideon. You can read the full story in Judges 6:1–40. It happened at a time when government in Israel was virtually non-existent. There was no regular administrative system, but from time to time when crises arose, usually from hostile neighboring tribes, the people were forced to look for leadership. During these periods God graciously provided just-the-right people, eccentric though some of them must have been, to act as leaders. They were known as judges.

Gideon was called upon to act in that capacity during one such crisis. From the Midianites and other tribes, the Israelites faced an external threat so severe that most people fled the farmlands and took flight into the hills. Every crop they grew was devastated by marauding enemies, but they faced an even greater threat that was internal. They had turned their backs on God, and this oppression by Midian was God's way of disciplining them for worshiping false deities. Eventually the Israelites came to their senses and realized what was happening. It was then they began to pray. God in his grace heard them and stepped in to set them free once more from oppression, but he needed someone to lead them to this freedom by fighting the Midianites. It is there that Gideon entered the story.

Gideon had an unenviable task. God required the people to repent if they were to be given deliverance, but then, as now, the people wanted to be free without really changing their ways. So Gideon had a fair amount of opposition to face and overcome from his own people before he could turn to face the Midianites. No wonder he needed much encouragement!

As he often is, God was extraordinarily understanding of Gideon's need and sent an angel to encourage him (Judges 6:11). Apparently Gideon was not quick on the uptake, for not until he had prepared a meal for his companion did he realize that he had just spent the previous hour discussing the current state of affairs in Israel with an angel! He realized that his companion had not dived into the food as an ordinary, hungry person would, but had touched it with the tip of the staff he was carrying, and fire flared out of the rock and consumed it.

As if this sign were not enough to encourage Gideon to believe he had rightly understood the call of God to deliver Israel, God gave him another sign. It happened like this: Gideon courageously took a stand against false religion and one night demolished an idol to Baal and a sacred pole connected with the worship of Asherah, substituting a proper altar to God in their place. When this action was discovered the next morning, the lynch mob got busy and went in search of Gideon. Surprisingly, however, they listened to some common sense about whether Baal really was a god able to look after himself and so withheld attacking Gideon's house. It was nothing short of a miracle. Surely this, too, would have confirmed to Gideon that God was on his side and that he had not mistaken the Voice he heard calling him to fight the Midianites.

Yet he still needed reassurance. Before he ventured further, he went to God again and asked for one more sign to make sure that he had gotten his guidance right. This is where the fleece became involved.

Gideon asked God for a miraculous, circumstantial sign. He would leave a woolen fleece on the ground that night and if, when he examined it the next morning, the fleece was wet with dew while the ground all around was dry, he would accept that God was with him and he was to defeat the Midianites. In a matter-of-fact way the Bible simply records, "And that is what happened."

Nevertheless, Gideon was still not content. Although he realized that he was near to trying God's patience, if he had not already done so, he asked God for yet one more experimental sign. Perhaps he had second thoughts about the first sign with the fleece. Perhaps he realized that if a woolen fleece is left out on dewy grass, it is likely to absorb the dew around it and leave the surrounding earth dry. It would be much more difficult for this to happen by chance the other way around, so he begged God to repeat the action, only this time in the reverse direction. This time could God arrange for the ground to be wet but the fleece to be dry? Then he would be sure. We are not told what God might have said about Gideon to his companions in heaven. Again in a matter-of-fact way we are simply told, "That night God did so."

On the foundation of this story people have built a superstructure concerning guidance. Many have asked God to give them guidance through a circumstantial sign and called it "putting out a fleece." Today people are usually asking God for signs that are possible if not actually probable. How we weight the sign on the scale of probability usually depends on how much we want to receive a positive answer from God. So we say, "If the Buffalo Bills win on Saturday, I'll go to the mission field." "If the phone rings in the next half hour I'll give twenty bucks to the Red Cross." "If the next bus to pass me is red, I'll go and visit old Mrs. Posslethwaite on the way home tonight." And so on.

ON THE ONE HAND

There are two things to be said in Gideon's favor.

First, asking God to perform this sign showed that Gideon had a right worldview. A worldview is a framework by which we interpret the world around us. He believed in a personal God quite capable of intervening in the world and arranging things for his own ends. After all, it was his world. Gideon believed in the possibility of the miraculous. In this he differed from many of his contemporaries. Those who worshiped Baal did not believe in such a god. For them the impersonal forces of nature were in control and although people had to placate them by rituals and sacrifices in order to secure a good harvest, none of their so-called gods and goddesses were like the God Gideon knew. His God was one with whom mankind could have a personal and gracious relationship and one who would use his sovereign power for gracious ends. So, Gideon had a right belief in God although that did not necessarily mean that it was right to believe that God would intervene miraculously when Gideon so desired.

The second thing that Gideon had in his favor was that he showed a right understanding of what he was asking God to do. He saw the danger of the first sign he had asked for—it was too possible and more than likely to happen—so he changed it. He had integrity and was careful not to predetermine the results.

ON THE OTHER HAND

Having said that, there were severe problems then with using this form of guidance, and there still are. They are so severe that one much respected Christian leader, John White, says bluntly, "Forget about fleeces. If you've never used them, don't start. If you have, then quit." What are these problems?

There are eight problems to face.

First, if you resort to putting out a fleece you should ask yourself if you are really asking God for a miracle. That is what Gideon was consciously doing, and if we are using a Gideon's fleece we should not fall short of doing the same.

The problem is that we usually do not do anything of the sort when we claim to be putting out a fleece. We usually ask God to do something on the spectrum between the possible and the probable but not something that we regard as impossible or highly improbable. Thus, we are not operating in the realm of the miraculous.

Most often our requests to God fall in the 50–50 category. It may happen, or it may not. In that case, why not draw lots or toss a coin? There is more biblical precedent for doing this than there is for putting out a fleece. The outcome of casting lots is really beyond our control and safely in the hands of God.

The second problem arises simply because we are usually asking not for the miraculous but for something much more mundane to happen. The fact of the matter is that when we ask God to do a certain thing that is on the possible-probable spectrum, our perception changes. With a heightened sense of awareness we start looking for him to do what we have asked and so we see him do it. Then we claim the guidance we were seeking. If it were a miracle we were looking for, it would be an event that struck us as so unusual that we could be sure it was not just us seeing things we wanted to see but something that clearly God had done.

Just imagine you are seeking guidance as to whether you should apply yourself to saving for the car you have always dreamed of owning—a new BMW. You say to God that if you see more than five BMWs on your way to work the next day, you will take it as guidance that you should go ahead and work flat-out to achieve your goal. Lo and behold, on your way to work the next day you see not five but eight BMWs. Surely God has answered with abundant clarity! But hold on a moment. Those BMWs have probably always been there and probably more besides. More than likely, they registered in your subconscious before you asked God for this fleece. What has changed is not that God has suddenly produced five BMWs but that heightened senses have made you consciously register the existence of five BMWs within a twenty-mile radius.

It is not unusual, once you have bought a new car, to see new cars everywhere. Nor is it unusual once you have decided to move to a new town, to hear about it everywhere and to keep meeting people who grew up there. Actually all that has happened is that we have become aware of that car or that town in a way that previously had escaped us. Therefore, if it is a fleece we are after, we must be sure that it really is a sign from God and not just altered perception on our part.

The third problem is that, to be frank, Gideon's fleece was an expression of doubt and unbelief on his part. His confession that he is likely to be trying God's patience (Judges 6:37) admits as much. God had already sent him an angel and miraculously delivered him from an angry, violent mob, and he was still asking for guidance. If those earlier experiences had not convinced him, would he ever be sure?

Jesus warned the people of his time about constantly demanding signs from God (Matthew 12:39, 16:4). Asking for signs is sometimes a symptom of a stubborn and unbelieving heart. We are called to walk by faith not by sight, thus there must always be an element of trusting God and accepting his word without signs. Far from such a position of faith's being second best, Jesus declared such a position to be truly blessed (John 20:29).

Fourth, we must ask a bottom-line-type question. When Gideon had received the signs he asked for, was he any more sure of God's will than before? The fact that he asked God for a second sign suggests that he did not really grow in confidence of God's will after receiving the first sign.

Often that is the way it is. Rather than settling issues clearly, laying a fleece often just throws up a new set of doubts and questions. Suppose we determine that the phone should ring by 9:15 A.M. if we are to take a certain course of action, and it does not. Fine. But then suppose it does ring at 9:17 A.M. Does that count or not? And suppose you discover that the watch by which you were timing it is three minutes fast and what is 9:17 A.M. by your watch is really 9:14 A.M. Or assume that you want a letter by Tuesday morning if a certain course of action is to follow, but no letter comes when you go off to work that morning—then one comes by afternoon delivery and is waiting for you on your return. What are you to do?

It may all sound quite trivial, but these are just in the cascade of questions that descends, and this is just the welter of uncertainty that people enter when they go down this road. I know this because countless people have confessed it. The really serious concern is that it implies a small image of God. It seems to suggest that he likes playing a game of trivial pursuits with us.

Talking of God's nature leads us to a fifth problem. The request that God guide us through a fleece may cause us to dishonor God by reducing him. We may be in danger of treating God as if he were our puppet. What we may be doing is to say to God, "Please God, jump into my box and perform for me." This is the other side, the dark side, of believing in a

God of the miraculous. The danger is that we lose respect and reverence for him. We come to him without awe, asking him to do things that are convenient for us, without any sense of his sovereignty, his greatness or his majesty. We end up, if we are not very careful, "using" God.

The sixth problem about the way we use fleeces emerges if we look honestly at what Gideon was doing. He put out his fleece so that God could give him confirmation of a decision he had, in fact, already made. It was not actually a way of making the decision in the first place. We sometimes use the fleece as a way of making decisions rather than confirming them, and in doing so we abdicate responsibility for the decisions we are making. And that is not a mature way of behavior.

There may well be a place for doing just what Gideon did, that is, of asking God, once we have made a decision, for gracious confirmation by some sort of sign. I have known God to do that in my own life, and I acknowledge it with gratitude. But that is a different matter from asking God to make your mind up for you by means of a sign, and it is not what most people today mean by laying a fleece.

Seventh, we must recognize that Gideon did not have all the resources available to him that we have available to us. We have already spoken of some of the resources God has given us, such as the Holy Spirit and the Bible. Perhaps it was more necessary for Gideon to resort to other means of guidance in days when spiritual resources were more sparse. On the whole, we should not have to do so.

The eighth objection is this: Laying a fleece is not a method of guidance practiced anywhere else in the Bible with the possible exception of Genesis 24:14, when Abraham's servant was choosing a bride for Isaac. Nowhere else is it commended, and it is certainly never commended as a way of seeking God's guidance. The New Testament is silent on the issue. In fact, the weight of the Bible's teaching should make us cautious. On many occasions, including Numbers 20, Deuteronomy 32, and the teaching of Jesus already mentioned, there are clear warnings about putting God to the test by asking him to give a sign before we believe what he has said.

No wonder John White says, "Forget it."

ON THE THIRD HAND

I have a friend who cannot speak without using his hands to emphasize or clarify the point. Being a lecturer, he uses his hands a great deal. His lectures are peppered with "on the one hand" and "on the other hand." In fact, it seems to me as I listen to him that two hands are never enough. He really needs a third, fourth, and fifth hand to develop his theme. In that manner we come to the third hand.

The heavy catalog of problems we have detailed about the fleece needs to be put in perspective. Using a fleece as a way of finding God's guidance is not the worst sin imaginable! It is just that it is likely to lead to all sorts of pastoral problems. But before we write it off, we need to acknowledge that there are two things in the history of Gideon that appear to be in its favor.

The plain fact is that, whatever our objections, God did answer Gideon. If it was so bad and such an expression of doubt, why did God do so? He did so because he is gracious. "As a father has compassion on his children, so the LORD has compassion on those who fear him; for he knows how we are formed, he remembers that we are dust" (Psalm 103:13–14). He knows our limitations and is understanding about our frailties. Just at that time Gideon was under severe strain. He was caught up in events that were traumatic and whose consequences were immense. The very future of the nation was at stake and, through no fault of his own, he was in the middle of it all. It is not surprising that God was gentle with him.

God's graciousness does not necessarily mean that Gideon's action was right—or that it will be right for us. When I was at university, in the dark ages, we suffered "formal dinners" twice a week. We were more enlightened than some colleges who had to suffer them every night, but even so, they seemed a relic from the past and we were eager to do away with them. Part of the problem with formal meals was that we were required to dress in suits and ties, and wear gowns. Some of the radical members of the college turned up on one occasion without their gowns, outrageously flouting the rules. It happened to be a night when the professors were descending from their high table to sit among the rebels. Later, when we were debating the wearing of gowns at a college meeting, the militants argued that the dean approved of their abolition or he would not have sat among them earlier at that formal dinner. "Not at all," protested the dean, "you misunderstand. I did not sit with you because I approved of your action, but because I wanted to learn to relate to you in spite of your disobedience." Such is the grace of God.

Finally, we must admit that seeking guidance in this way still sometimes seems to work. And why not? Sometimes God speaks to us this way and there is nothing more to add, but sometimes there is another way of understanding why it works.

Often it works because, in reality, we are not putting out a fleece at all. All that we are doing is setting out wise conditions on which to make a decision. We may say, "If I'm offered $9,000 for my car, I will sell it." Or, "If I get a doctorate degree, I'll do research." Or, "If ninety percent of the church invites me to work with them, I'll accept." The receipt of the $9,000, the gaining of the advanced degree, the call of the ninety percent are not really fleeces we have laid before God at all. They are all sensible conditions we have rightly thought through as the basis for our decisions. Hence, at the end of the day, we are often right back to the normal way God guides—through the making of wise decisions that are spiritually expedient.

Fleeces may well have their place as a way by which God will guide us, but we should use them rarely if at all, resorting to them only when we have thought through in some depth what we are asking God to do for us to ensure the maximum opportunity for God to show us his free and sovereign will.□

Chapter 7

Guidance at the Job Center

In this and the following two chapters we will be concerned with three big questions that fall in the area where the Christian has freedom to come to his own decisions. The questions are about work, marriage, and full-time Christian service.

According to the sociologists our world is "peculiarly open." By this they do not mean that you must watch your step lest at any moment you fall into some great black hole, nor are they commenting on the number of times the road is dug up by one of the public services. Believe it or not, they are talking about the course your life or mine might take. We can choose more freely from a greater range of options than any generation before us has ever been able to choose.

In previous generations a boy would follow his dad down into the mine, onto the land, or into the army and count himself lucky. He would not have thought to any serious extent about doing something different from his father's example. Girls would not have thought much at all about pursuing a career. The doors of choice were simply not open to them. A few occupations would have been available to those who were not yet married or who were destined to be single or poor, but otherwise women were not admitted much to gainful employment.

Once an occupation was undertaken, chances were that you would stay there for life. My grandfather was given a retirement gold (well, gold-leafed) watch by the Great Western Railway, for whom he had worked all his life. Company loyalty was prized. Such presentations were not uncommon in his day, but who hears of them now?

Many more of us, although by no means all, find our world much more open. We face numerous choices regarding subjects and options as to whether we stay or leave. When we do leave, we are faced with a bewildering variety of choices about courses and colleges; that is, if we look for further education at all. Once in a job we do not assume that we shall be there for life. Even if we do, we may find, like many who had no intention of leaving their work before retirement, that we are forced by the all-pervasive power of market forces to retrain, quite late in life, for something else. Therefore, if we want to switch horses midstream, we can—and may even have to, whether we want to or not.

All this makes the question of guidance much more urgent for us than for our forebears. It also perhaps explains why the Bible does not give the matter any extensive treatment. For people in the

Bible's world, choosing jobs and changing them was no more a question than was the matter of nuclear energy.

The passage that seems most helpful is in the middle of a long discussion about the merits of marriage, in 1 Corinthians 7:17–24. Three major principles emerge, all of which dovetail with the principles that we have set out earlier concerning guidance.

EVERY SITUATION IS A CALLING FROM GOD

Paul was writing to young Christians who had bombarded him with question after question about the Christian life. The question he puts in 1 Corinthians 7 is, "Is it preferable for Christians to remain single rather than marry?" There were several reasons why the question was posed. Some were simply anxious to do the best for God and wanted advice. Others were unhappily married to non-Christian husbands and were wistfully asking to see if there was a way out of their predicament. Still others were enthusiasts who thought the Lord was going to return at any moment, thus they had no time for the responsibilities imposed by marriage or family. Yet others probably thought that sex was dirty and so thought a "real" Christian would not get married.

In his reply, Paul gets them to look not only at the question of marriage but at some broader principles that relate to work as well. To begin with, he points out that for a Christian there is no one position that is superior to another. Marriage is a legitimate option for a Christian and so is singleness. Each state has its advantages and responsibilities and no one has the right to say one is above the other. The same is true with being circumcised or not being circumcised. Circumcision is no longer relevant to one's salvation, so there is nothing to boast about if you are circumcised and nothing to bemoan if you are not.

Paul then applies the same argument to the question of work. By the sound of it, some who had become Christians wanted to throw off their lowly status as slaves and were striving to gain their freedom. We cannot be sure whether this was from a general desire to make personal progress, arising from the richer appreciation of life that often comes when a person is converted and which those who study missions today call "redemption and lift," or whether it was more specific. Perhaps some who were slaves to Christian masters were arguing more radically that it was actually wrong that they should still be enslaved by their Christian brothers who were, after all, their spiritual equals. Either way, Paul sets out two important issues in reply. He writes, "Each one should remain in the situation which he was in when God called him. Were you a slave when you were called? Don't let it trouble you—although if you can gain your freedom, do so" (verses 20–21).

The first important issue is that all work is a calling from God. On the surface it may seem merely to be a way of earning enough money to pay the bills or even just a regrettable necessity. We may think we are trapped in our job by force of circumstances or even mishap. But the Christian must learn to think more deeply. It is God's providence that has put you there. Consequently, God's call to you is to learn to serve him and honor him where you are. This transfers our idea of work from the secular sphere and locates it in the realm of worship. God is involved in what you are doing now.

The second important issue is that no particular form of work is superior to another. There are some limitations to that statement that we shall make later in the chapter, but for the moment let us think about the wonder of it. The Corinthians were making the mistake of assessing the value of work according to secular standards. Worried about their social status, they did not like being slaves and bearing the stigma attached to their position. They would have preferred to be free and to enjoy the prestige of freedom, but Paul tells them they are not to be troubled by such considerations. God knew they were slaves when he called them, and called them just the same. He did not call them into his kingdom because they were socially more significant than others, because such considerations simply did not matter. Slaves were free to serve God in their slavery as much as masters were bound to serve him in their more liberated positions. "For he who was a slave when he was called by the Lord is the Lord's freedman; similarly, he who was a free man when he was called is Christ's slave" (verse 22).

Consider the following implications:

All work is sanctified and can be transformed into an act of service to God whether it be performed by the laborer, the farmer, the electronic engineer, the minister, or the road-construction worker.

It is not true that ministers, missionaries, and other full-time Christian workers are the "called" elite, whereas the rest can choose for themselves because they are in inferior occupations. Every one of us is "called by God," a point to which we shall return in chapter 9. All callings are of equal value to God and must be approached with the same degree of spiritual seriousness as one would expect from ministers or missionaries entering their vocations.

Paul also draws the implication that if every occupation is a calling from God then we should not strive to be free from it. Restless ambition is to be rejected. "Each one should retain the place in life that the Lord assigned to him and to which God has called him" (verse 17). There is no need to be anxious to be something else, for the simple reason that you are already somebody in Christ. It is impossible for the Christian to be "only a roadsweeper," or "only a computer programmer." There is no "only" about it, since the Christian has been given the highest status in Christ (verse 22).

An understanding of what Paul is teaching here should cause Christians to approach work differently from their co-workers who do not know Christ. The stress of ambition, the assumptions about promotion, the striving to get higher up the ladder should all be absent. It is not only that we reject materialism; it is that we judge people on a different basis from the way the world does. The world is concerned about titles, money, status, position, and work. We are not. We see people as either in Christ or not. If they are in Christ, they are equal brothers and sisters whatever their station in life is.

Paul's basic point then is: Learn to serve Christ where you are.

John Calvin has summed up the issues very well:

> The Lord enjoins every one of us, in all the actions of life, to have respect to our own calling. He knows the boiling restlessness of the human mind, the fickleness with which it is borne hither and thither, its eagerness to hold opposites at one time in its grasp, its ambition. Therefore, lest all things should be thrown into confusion by our folly and rashness, he has assigned distinct duties to each in the different modes of life. . . . Every man's mode of life, therefore, is a kind of station assigned him by the Lord, that he may not be always driven about at random.
> (*Institutes of the Christian Religion*, III, 10:6)

FREE CHOICE IS AN OPTION FROM GOD

With that as an anchor point we can now look at the second principle.

Is Paul really saying that Christians must never go for promotion, or that if the Corinthian slaves were offered their freedom they should reject it? How does Paul's advice help when one is unemployed, or seeking to find God's guidance about facing several open doors, or being encouraged to go for promotion?

It is here his second principle helps. The principle is that as far as occupations are concerned, Christians are encouraged to accept the opportunities given to them. Verse 21 says, "Although if you can gain your freedom, do so." God does not want to keep Christians down so that they always occupy the lowest rungs of the occupational ladder. There is no command to remain in slavery if the possibility of release is offered. Instead, the Christian is encouraged to accept the opportunities that God allows to come his way. Accordingly, says Paul, if the choice is there and freedom is offered, accept it.

We can only guess what Paul would make of our "peculiarly open" society in which many of us face far more opportunities than we can fulfill. It would seem from the specific issue he is dealing with here that he would not find it a problem but would rejoice at the variety of options we face. He would dare us to believe that such choice was of God and encourage us to use our own minds to come to decisions as to which options we are going to pursue. It is an area in which the Christian has liberty to choose as he wishes to.

We must be thankful that any number of Christians have seen it this way and risen right to the top of their professions or their country, and, as a result, have been able to exercise great influence for Christ in those positions. But equally we must respect the right of others not to assume they must automatically accept promotion when it is offered to them. It is no freedom to be trapped in the rat race and to allow some tyrannical profession or totalitarian employer to predetermine our course in life and our daily path for us. Freedom means freedom to say no as much as freedom to say yes.

In writing this, we assume that we shall reach our decisions according to the principles already outlined.

They will, therefore, be wise decisions. In fact, Paul gives us further help at this point because in the verses surrounding those we have just examined he spells out some of the factors that will make our decisions wise or foolish.

BASIC PRINCIPLES IN LIVING FOR GOD

Paul mentions four basic factors that will help us to choose our occupations wisely. In practice we do not have *carte blanche* as the second principle, taken on its own, would suggest. In considering which job we go for, we must bear in mind these additional things.

Obedience to the Commandments

Having said that circumcision and uncircumcision are irrelevant to the Christian, Paul goes on bluntly to say, "Keeping God's commands is what counts" (verse 19).

This must immediately mean that certain occupations are not open to the Christian and there cannot be any discussion about it. To be a thief is to break the commandments, thus no Christian can support himself that way. Likewise, while it may not entail the owner in committing adultery himself, running a brothel provides the opportunity for others to do so, and therefore is breaking the commandments, at least by proxy.

Wisdom would suggest that our concern must not only be to keep the letter of the law but its spirit, too. Consequently, we should want to give a wide berth to certain occupations, which, although they may not be directly condemned in the Ten Commandments, clearly violate the holy heart of God. It is difficult to see, for example, that Christians can with an easy conscience be involved in trades related to gambling. Slot machines are a social evil that have destroyed many young lives with their addictive powers, and serve no socially useful purpose. I was not surprised when a recent convert in my church, who had told me he was going to set up a slot machine business, came back a week later to tell me he was not going to do so any longer. I had not mentioned the matter to him—there were too many other things to talk about at the time—but the Spirit had taught him how wrong it would have been.

A whole range of occupations become suspect on this basis, some more so than others. Certain businesses trade on people's weaknesses and rejoice when those who are vulnerable get into debt. Others are involved in the destruction of God's creation, either militarily or to satisfy the hunger of the overfed west. Others, such as the alcohol trade or the tobacco industry, inevitably contribute to many injuries and problems, and even death. All these are occupations about which, Christians must think deeply as to how they square with the commandments before they enter them or wish to remain in them.

A positive concern to obey the commandments will lead to a person's choosing a socially useful and beneficial occupation. It is not surprising that many Christians have wanted to get involved in education or the caring professions. That is how it should be.

Likewise, manufacturing and creating *honest* wealth are socially beneficial occupations. Obeying the commandments involves not only avoiding what is wrong but doing what is good.

Slavery to Christ

Paul is concerned to release Christians from human slavery, but in doing so reminds them that they are in fact bound by a greater slavery since they are the Lord's slaves, "bought at a price" (verse 23). He is repeating what he told them only a short while before in 1 Corinthians 6:19–20, "You are not your own; you were bought at a price. Therefore honor God with your body." There it applied to their sexual lives. Here the same principle was applied to their social and occupational status.

Freed from human and social tyranny, Christians have put themselves under a new master. Paradoxically, it is through serving him that they find their perfect freedom. That master is Christ.

Consequently, when it comes to questions of work and employment, the basic question all Christians should ask is, "What does my master want me to do?" You can, of course, only get to know his will by close involvement with him. A careful study of the Gospels, enabling you to hear his concerns and discover his priorities, would be a good starting point. The relationship would build from there.

If you do get to know him in this way, then his compassion for the poor, his reaching out to the lost, his opposing of evil, and his desire for his disciples to go and make other disciples on a worldwide scale is an agenda you will not fail to see. If you have freedom, gift, and opportunity, this agenda may be one to which you contribute. But if not, the Gospels will tell you how to work and relate in the workplace in a way that will show whose servant you are.

When it comes to your next job application, remember that you are a servant of Jesus Christ. What would your master say about it?

Freedom from People

Paul well understands this is a radical claim to impose on people. It is radical not only because of what it says about slavery to Christ, but equally because of what it says about freedom from the world. It cuts Christians loose from the world's values and assessments.

In Paul's day the key criterion by which one evaluated another's worth was whether or not he was circumcised, if one was a Jew, or whether or not one was a slave, if a Gentile. Today the world has a different checklist.

Now the world assesses others' importance by whether or not they are employed or in a profession or a trade; whether they are rich or poor; by their title, the size of their bank balance, their position in the company, or even whether or not they are married.

Christians think altogether differently, or rather should. Such worldly estimations are of no relevance in assessing the value of a person in Christ. Yet, so many of us betray the fact that we really still assess people by worldly standards. A former colleague used to fake people out beautifully. It would be funny, if it were not so serious. She worked on the staff of the Bible college and remarked on people's reaction when they were introduced to her. Most made the automatic assumption that she worked in the kitchen or on the cleaning staff, or perhaps, at most, was a secretary. She used sometimes to string them along and pretend that she was. She soon found that people were not too interested in a cook or a cleaner, and conversations usually came to a quick end. As soon as she revealed her real identity as a superbly qualified lecturer, however, the tone of the conversation changed. People became much more interested and started kowtowing, as well! Perhaps the church is not so free from slavery to the world system as it ought to be!

The way you approach finding your next job is likely to show just which master you really serve. Are you a slave of Christ or of the world?

Responsible to God

It is only a passing phrase, but it is there nonetheless. What dynamite it contains! In verse 24 where Paul is encouraging people to stay in their present positions he writes in parenthesis, "as responsible to God."

All Christians are accountable to God for what they have done with this precious gift of life that he has given them. When we stand before him on the judgment day as Christians no less than others will do, will we be thrilled or ashamed at what we have done with our lives?

Jesus himself warned us that we shall be accountable to God in the parable of the talents (Matthew 25:14–30). Paul underlined it in 2 Corinthians 5:10, "For we must all appear before the judgment seat of Christ, that each one may receive what is due him for the things done while in the body, whether good or bad." And that includes not just whether we have been kind in helping older persons to cross the road but what we did with our jobs, which is where we spend the major proportion of our time. At school many of us earned the comment on our work, "could do better." It would be a shame to receive that as the final comment on our lives from our Maker.

There may be no signposts telling us individually, explicitly, and in glorious technicolor whether or not we should accept one job or apply for another. But there are some very clear principles that should shape our thinking on the matter.

So how do Christians go about finding God's guidance concerning work? First, they must check escapism and honestly ask whether they are already serving God well in the position they are in. Second, they must shun restlessness and blatant striving to better themselves. That is the world's agenda. Third, they must welcome the opportunities that come their way as gifts of God. Fourth, they must exercise their freedom to choose wisely, providing that they always remember that they are to obey the commandments, that they are slaves of Christ, that they are to be free from the world, and that they are responsible to God.

If those principles are genuinely observed, then we may choose what we will.□

Chapter 8

Take Your Partners, Please

Apart from conversion, getting married is the biggest step of faith anyone is likely to take. There are enough uncertainties built into marriage without unnecessarily inviting more. It is not surprising, therefore, that many should want to know if their partner is the Lord's "Mr. Right" or "Miss Right" for them before they propose. How can they be sure?

By now we probably realize that there is no way we can thumb through our Bibles and find a text that says, "Marry Cynthia" or "Propose to Bill." The Bible does not speak directly about *our* particular case. We can only start with the general principles it does give us and build from there.

GENERAL PRINCIPLES ABOUT MARRIAGE

To Marry or Not to Marry?

It may seem strange to begin a section on "general principles about marriage" with the question of singleness, but perhaps that just betrays our lack of knowledge of the Bible. God invented marriage so that a person might overcome loneliness (Genesis 2:18). It might therefore be taken for granted that marriage is usually God's intention for his children, but that does not mean that it is always right. For some people, remaining single is a quite right and proper thing to do before God.

Jesus himself was the most perfect human being in history and yet he was single. Marriage cannot, therefore, be essential to being a complete person. He acknowledged that some will renounce marriage "because of the kingdom of heaven" (Matthew 19:12) and pointed out that marriage was only a provisional arrangement on earth since, "At the resurrection people will neither marry nor be given in marriage; they will be like the angels" (Matthew 22:30). Paul spoke of singleness as a spiritual gift (1 Corinthians 7:7) and told the Corinthians of the advantages that there were in being single. Single people are free from the family responsibilities that marriage imposes on those who enter it. They are, therefore, in a better position to be single-minded about the work of the Lord than married folk are (1 Corinthians 7:29–35).

The Bible sets out three reasons why people might remain single. The first might be termed *congenital*: "for some are eunuchs because they were born that way" (Matthew 19:12). These have some physical or psychological disability that makes marriage difficult, but never, by God's grace, impossible. The second reason is *circumstantial*. Jesus goes on to say that "others were made that way by men." A whole range of issues make up those circumstances: No one ever proposed; parents forbade it; careers took over; the demands of looking after elderly relatives prevented it; there was just no opportunity to find a partner; or marriage took place but it was sadly followed by divorce or bereavement.

Society tends to think of these two causes as the only causes and often looks with suspicion on the single person. But Jesus adds a third reason for some to remain single—that of wholesome *choice:* Some "have renounced marriage bcause of the kingdom of heaven." So we readily agree with Richard Foster in his book *Money, Sex, and Power* when he writes, "We do people a disservice when we fail to proclaim the single life as a positive Christian option. Marriage is not for everyone and we should say so!"

People can be happy and single just as they can be happy and married. It is, for some, a wholesome gift of the Spirit enabling them to use their freedom from a particular family to adopt a wide family, or their independence to be complete and joyful persons in the service of the Lord. Singleness does not have to be a burden. It can be enjoyed and does not necessarily have to be endured. This remains true even if people long to marry but the opportunity is denied them. The unsought-after circumstances may well be God's way of providing you with powerful guidance. Whether singleness is a burden or a blessing depends, as in the case of many other things in life, on one's attitude. Wisdom leads one to accept it rather than to fight it, and to yield it to God, allowing him to work through it. Many persons who may have felt left on the shelf have discovered that with right attitudes God may yet bring about their wish. But if he does not, it no longer matters.

Yet we must be realistic and recognize that there are particular stresses that a single person faces. Single people remain sexual people, but unless they can discipline their sexual drive and avoid falling into temptation, Paul argues that it is better for them to direct their sexual desires into the channel of marriage as God intended than to fall into sin (1 Corinthians 7:9). Besides, there are other needs a single person might have. There are the needs of companionship, affection, communication, protection, and a host of other personal needs. The single state is not easy, especially in a society in which much social pressure is put on single persons to conform to the more statistically normal family type.

Consider with care the question of whether to marry or not to marry, therefore. Christians should not automatically assume the right to marry, even though it might be more usual. The calling of God for some might well be to remain single. We must certainly thank God for many who have done so down through the years and given themselves unstintingly to the work of Christ both at home and overseas. The church would have been much the poorer without them and so would humanity. Singleness is therefore a valid option before God, but if you decide it is for you, seek the grace of God that you might not only be fulfilled but kept pure.

The Nature and Purpose of Marriage

Supposing you have evaluated that question and still feel it right to marry, what other general principles come into play? The next important thing to know is what God says about the purpose and nature of marriage. The basis for it is in Genesis 2:18 and 24. The primary purpose of marriage is companionship. It involves a person's separating from his or her parents and setting up a new family unit. In that new relationship the couple are expected by God to "be united" to each other and become one flesh; that is, to engage in sexual intercourse and have children (Genesis 2:24). In amplifying these words, Jesus makes it clear that what is expected is that a couple will enter into a lifelong union in which a husband and wife will hold fast only to each other in a relationship that terminates when one of them dies (Matthew 19:1–9). It may seem strange that Genesis concludes this section by saying, "The man and his wife were both naked, and they felt no shame" (Genesis 2:25), but actually it is a natural follow-up since complete openness, complete trust, and complete intimacy should be the marks of marriage.

We may translate these general principles about the purpose and nature of marriage into a number of very practical questions that test one's readiness for it. Those who fail the test are not therefore ruled out from getting married, but it may suggest there is some further learning or growing up to be done before embarking on it.

Those about to enter marriage ought to be able to

give some evidence of being able to cope with living away from home and making their own decisions. There ought to be some ability to give and receive love, although not to the extent that it has been tested out in premarital sexual intercourse. There should be signs that the couple are ready to enter into a lifelong commitment and are responsible enough to keep such an awesome promise. The ability to talk about issues such as finance, dreams for the future, children, should be present, as should the ability to resolve conflict and to adapt to living together.

Areas of Compatibility

Marriage involves the complete sharing of oneself with another. That means that there needs to be compatibility between the partners. Compatibility does not mean that they have to think alike in everything. That would be boring. Part of the purpose is for one partner to stimulate the other so that each becomes a richer and fuller person through marriage. Complementarity, rather than complete imitation, is what is called for.

That complementarity needs to take place in at least four areas. First, there is the personal area. Do the couple find it easy to talk and share things in common? Do they have enough in common to enjoy doing things together and enough differences to lead the other into new areas? Do they share enough similarity of outlook so that home is not always going to be a battlefield? And enough differences so that they are not simply going to agree with each other?

Second, there must be social complementarity. There are no iron laws in operation, determining which marriages succeed and which fail. Even so, we know that the chances of a marriage breaking up are increased if people from different social backgrounds marry. Often this means that there is just not enough in common for people to build on. Ideas of entertainment, of child-rearing, of communication, of handling finance, of relating to the wider family, of holidays, and a host of other things are all to some extent shaped by our social background. Social compatibility, therefore, helps.

Third, there is need for physical compatibility. The Bible teaches that one should reserve the act of sexual intercourse for marriage itself (1 Thessalonians 4:3–8; Hebrews 13:4). One cannot therefore finally know about physical compatibility until after marriage. But then, it is equally true that in the other areas, too, there is so much one does not discover until after the marriage has taken place and the couple are actually living together, so it is not really different from those areas. With that qualification it is fair to ask if the couple find each other physically attractive and stimulating. This is an important aspect of the relationship and should not be underestimated.

The final area is the spiritual area. Is there also compatibility here? Because marriage is the complete sharing of oneself with another, it is wholly unwise for a Christian to enter into a marriage relationship with a non-Christian. Those who do, enter into a relationship where a major area of significance cannot be shared. For this reason, both in 1 Corinthians 7:39

and 2 Corinthians 6:14–18, Paul makes it abundantly clear that Christians should only marry Christians.

In Summary . . . .

The Bible's teaching about marriage is much fuller than we have set out here. The point has not been to expound it all and give a complete marriage preparation course but to select those parts that relate to the question of how one finds one's partner. The general principles have shown us that:

1. We must consider whether it is right to marry or remain single.
2. We must understand the nature and purpose of marriage, which may lead us to question whether it is the right time to get married.
3. We must recognize the need for personal, social, physical, and spiritual compatibility in marriage, which rules out a Christian from marrying an unbeliever.

YES, BUT WHO?

Some may have read the above with some impatience. They are itching to get to the more interesting question of whether Jane or Mary or indeed anyone is the *right* wife for them. The difficulty is that there is no shortcut to that question.

The general principles will have ruled out certain people as suitable partners. They should, for example, have given strong discouragement to any Christian thinking of marrying a non-Christian. They have told us what the will of God is for us in terms of how God wants us to live morally and spiritually. But that may still leave us with a wide choice and a number of options. There may still be several potential marriage partners who are Christians with whom we are spiritually compatible and who are ready for marriage. How are we to be guided to God's choice?

Checking Your Perspective

Our problem lies once more in our perspective. We seem to think there is a divine dating agency by which we have all been matched up. The problem is to find out—with whom? It stems from our general belief that God has a plan for our lives, and specifically one as to whom we should marry and somehow we must wrest it from him. Our purpose in seeking guidance, or so we think, is to hit upon God's choice for us. Only then can we be sure that we have married "Miss" or Mr. Right." This approach brings into sharp focus the problems, outlined in chapter three, of our fixation with finding the plan of God for our life.

I have known a string of fellows paralyzed into inactivity, missing good opportunities, and dangling girls on the end of an endless piece of string, all because they did not want to go against God's will and make the wrong choice. They were scared that in choosing they might make a mistake and condemn themselves to live with God's second or even third choice for them, but not his first. Consequently, they have made no choice at all!

For most of them it has been a big decision that has been center stage in their prayer life for ages. Other things that required urgent intercession and should have found space in their prayers were crowded out until this one was answered. Relationships have been handled with immaturity, causing pain to potential partners. Most of all, they have had no way of discerning which of the two or three candidates they should possibly choose. That's not meant to sound chauvinistic. It is meant to capture realistically what goes on!

These problems are the result of having a wrong perspective about guidance. If we have questioned the whole idea of our being concerned about finding the individual will of God for our lives in general, we certainly need to do so specifically when it comes to finding a marriage partner. The Bible does not teach that there is one "Miss" or "Mr. Right" reserved exclusively by the angels for us and that we must play guessing games with God to find out who it is.

The Bible does teach that this, along with many other personal matters, falls within the area of freedom in which we must choose for ourselves, making our decision on the basis of the guidelines we outlined in Chapter 4. That means we must choose, using our minds with all their renewed abilities working on full power; it is, after all, a major choice that we are about to make and one that will affect us more than any other in life. It means we must choose prayerfully and humbly, considerately and thoughtfully, carefully and wisely for ourselves. This is consistent with the whole tenor of Paul's teaching about marriage in 1 Corinthians 7 that stresses our freedom to act as we choose to do so before the Lord.

The Generosity of God

The fact is that there may be more than one suitable partner for us. Once we have ruled out those who contravene the general principles we have outlined, there may well still be more than one potential partner left. For instance, Vivian and Julie might both have much to commend them. Both are legitimate options before God.

Jay Adams put it well, using an interesting illustration, when he wrote:

> God is the God of abundance. There are twelve baskets full of pieces of bread left over. In life's decisions, God doesn't always bring us into places where all choices are between right and wrong. In his greatness, his children often find themselves in the enviable position of choosing among two or more rights! It would have been right to take any one of the pieces of bread that Christ multiplied.

Suppose, for argument's sake, that you do not know whether to marry Vivian or Julie, how do you come to a wise choice in this area?

A wise choice means committing the matter to God in prayer.

A wise choice also means asking a number of important questions about your relationship with both Vivian and Julie.

Whose company do you enjoy the most, and why?

Remember, in asking this question, that you are not thinking of going to a holiday camp together but of building a home. What it means to enjoy one another may take on a different complexion from the enjoyment you have felt in sharing holidays together. With whom are you most relaxed? Remember that openness, trust, intimacy, and affection are going to be involved. Who enriches you most? It is probably not the one who says yes to you all the time but the one who questions, discusses, and challenges you to look at things afresh. Whose life will you enrich the most and enable to grow to her full, God-given potential as a person? Which one is most healthy to you spiritually? It does not matter if you are not in total agreement about the finer points of the Second Coming, or even how many Isaiahs there might have been. But can you pray together, talk of the things of God together, and do you have a common concern to serve God in some way? With which of the two do you feel most compatible? Which one will enable you to grow to maturity most? And, in case all that sounds dreadfully rational and cerebral, which one do you love most? Which makes your heart miss a beat and your pulse leap into action?

To this we need to add another factor. Love is blind, say the cynics. The problem is that sometimes their judgment is correct. Thus, in this area it is certainly worth listening to the honest comments of your friends and family. They have no right to exercise a veto on your decision. When married, you will leave the family nest and set up on your own, so it must be your decision. Yet, they can often see things you cannot see and may even have greater experience that is worth tapping. If it is generally true that, "The way of a fool seems right to him, but a wise man listens to advice" (Proverbs 12:15), then it is certainly true when it comes to marriage.

A DIFFERENT QUESTION

Assume, for argument's sake, that the question is different. Perhaps the question is not one of choice between one or more possible partners but rather, between a partner you are just not sure is the right one for you to move forward to marriage with or not. Perhaps if you wait longer, God may have someone else in mind. How do you then come to a wise decision?

Lying behind this question may well be the concern as to whether you are ready for marriage or not. It is a big decision and will have a profound impact on your lifestyle. You will no longer live as an individual but will always have to think for two. You will no longer have independence, or privacy. After marriage you should never be alone. Money, interests, leisure, holidays, house, bed, maybe even your car, and a good many other things will be shared constantly with the same person. You will not pick and choose whom you do things with in the same way ever again. It is worth taking time to get the decision right.

In spite of the immensity of the decision, do not let that pressure you into putting off making it. Millions have made it and have found joy beyond measure as a result, so it cannot be quite so dreadful as you fear. It can be the gateway to unimagined pleasure and blessing. Thousands make the decision every year and they survive. Another reason that some people are daunted by it is that currently one in every four marriages breaks down and a great deal of publicity is given to that phenomenon and the damage it causes. But do not let that frighten you. Remember that the reverse is also true: Three in every four marriages do not break down. These are natural apprehensions but not serious blockages to marriage.

More likely, the real cause of your anxiety arises from wondering whether or not you are personally ready to take such a step. Only by wise but not introspective examination can you come to a conclusion on the matter. A number of questions may give an indication as to how ready you are. But these should be treated with caution and not used as an examination paper on which you must pass every question or else fail the test.

Among the questions, in no particular order, are these:

> Do you make important decisions for yourself, independent of your parents?
> How will you cope with living away from home?
> Are you good at communicating with each other?
> Are you embarrassed or uneasy at giving and receiving affection?
> Have you a basic understanding of sex?

Can you talk with your partner about having children?

Can you manage your money well?

Can you postpone immediate wants for later enjoyments?

What role would you play in the home and what would you expect your partner to do?

What do you and your partner argue about? Is it fundamental and how do you manage conflict?

Is your image of marriage romantic or realistic?

What is your expectation of marriage?

How do you view each other's occupational futures?

Is there a common understanding of how to relate to your parents?

Have you committed your relationship to God?

Have you thought what each other will be like in forty years' time, and does that diminish your enthusiasm?

Why do you want to get married?

For many, one of the big stumbling blocks is uncertainty about the immediate future. Halfway through an apprenticeship with little money coming in, or halfway through a college course without any clear understanding of what happens next, does not seem an ideal time to enter a lifetime's commitment. I agree. And yet, surprising as it may seem, many have done so without any major difficulties. Caution ought to be balanced by the thought that marriage may never seem particularly opportune. It may always seem to be an interruption to the demands of a career or just the wrong moment because your next step is uncertain. A good marriage will, however, be able to master both those obstacles and may well provide you with a security and strength that enables you to cope even better with studies, career demands, or uncertainty than you could on your own.

Another form that uncertainty takes is the nagging doubt that if you wait a little longer, someone better will come along; someone who will match your dreams, or keep you rich, or make you zing in a way no one yet has. Usually such ambition arises from notions that are unrealistically romantic. They often have a tinge of arrogance about them, too. More often than not, the person who has such high standards is likely never to be satisfied. Occasionally the urge to delay is wise, often because of the limited circumstances in which a person lives. But if this is true, motives should be carefully examined.

There are no easy answers. You alone can tell when you are ready. In all this you are trying to work out living as a Christian when God has given you no set answers. The best you can do, therefore, is to use your renewed mind and allow God to form your thoughts through it.

God will guide you to your partner when you apply the general rules for making wise decisions to the specific area of marriage. It falls, like so many other issues, in the area of freedom, when, providing you are not breaking God's revealed will, he allows

139

you to choose with your Christian mind since he has not revealed specifically what you should do.

In this vital decision you must trust in the providence of God. He rules over all the affairs of our lives, and his sovereign will shall be done. But he normally chooses to do it not directly, as if he employed some heavenly dating agency that had an infallible computer with which to match people perfectly, but through us, indirectly, using the faculties he has given us that we have brought in submission to him. Therefore, let your actions and your choice show that you believe your life is being guided, all unseen, by God, and do not fear.□

Chapter 9

Feeling Called?

So you feel called to Christian work and you want to know how to go about it. Fine. It is a tremendous privilege to be involved in Christian service as one's full-time occupation. It is also a tremendous responsibility. In nursing, you may have the care of people's physical lives in your hands; in finance, it may be their material security. In driving, you will have the responsibility for their physical safety; and in building, you may have the care of their family comfort in your hands. But in Christian work you will have the care of their eternal destinies and spiritual well-being in your hands. We must therefore approach Christian service with caution.

IS THERE A SPECIAL CALLING?

Before we turn to some practical advice, it may be worthwhile to look at some very basic issues about being called to Christian service.

141

If you have mentioned your leading to anyone, you may have received an unexpected reaction, depending on how sensitive your friends are. Some people have been met with the blunt reply that we are all "called" and there is nothing special about their leading, since we are all called to serve Christ.

There is much truth in this. The New Testament frequently speaks of Christians as people who are "called." They are "called to belong to Jesus Christ" (Romans 1:6), "called to be saints" (Romans 1:7), "called to be holy" (1 Corinthians 1:2), "called to one hope" (Ephesians 4:4) and called to much more besides. The very idea of a calling implies that those who have been called have certain obligations to meet and standards to keep. So they are urged "to live a life worthy of the calling" they have received (Ephesians 4:1) and to recognize that their calling gives them a freedom, although it is a freedom that leads them to serve others (Galatians 5:13).

So we must affirm that every Christian, and not just full-time Christian workers, are people who are called to serve. Furthermore, we must welcome the emphasis on this that has been given in recent years in contrast to the stress on the role of the professional clergyman that has often existed in the past, as if others had nothing to offer. Every member of the church is gifted and has a contribution to make to its ministry and mission (Ephesians 4:7–13; 1 Peter 4:10). Only as we acknowledge this emphasis, can we make any sense of Paul's teaching that the church is a body in which even the most modest member has a significant part to play (1 Corinthians 12:12–31).

In what sense, then, are some people given a special calling to Christian work? The Bible gives us at least two insights into this. First, we see that Paul felt he had a special calling that was distinct from the calling of every Christian. It was a calling, in his case, "to be an apostle and set apart for the gospel of God" (Romans 1:1). He seems here to be particularly marking out his calling as different from the calling that comes to every believer, which he mentions just a few verses later in verse 5. None of us can be called to be apostles in the sense in which Paul was, but many of us can still be set apart for the gospel; that is, to preach it and teach it.

Second, we know that there were several people, like Timothy, who devoted themselves to full-time service for Christ, and that those who were set apart in this special way had the right to expect the church to support them and relieve them of the pressure of having to raise their income by working as well in the ordinary job market. Ironically, we learn about this because Paul did not want to use that right himself but chose instead to earn his own living by maintaining his old job as a tentmaker. Nonetheless, he insists that "those who preach the gospel should receive their living from the gospel" (1 Corinthians 9:14). So there were full-time Christian workers who were called and supported in that special way. These were the New Testament equivalents of the Old Testament priests and Levites who had long been the full-time paid religious leaders of the nation.

This means that from the beginning, the church has to be vitally involved in anyone's calling to full-time Christian service. Stating it bluntly, if they are expected to pay the bill, they have a right, out of Christian courtesy at least, to be consulted. This has not always been the case. The privilege of being supported in Christian work has been abused from the earliest days of the church and still is. An early Christian writing called the *Didache* warned its readers to be suspicious of those who wandered into their fellowships, unknown and unproven, and demanded support just because they were traveling preachers.

The danger has multiplied today when Christian societies of all shapes and sizes have mushroomed and all of them demand financial support. Sometimes one cannot help but feel that their existence owes more to the desire of their founders to escape the pressures of earning their own wage in the everyday world, or to their desire to indulge a personal hobby without being accountable to anyone, than to the preaching of the gospel. If the church is to offer support, then the worker must be prepared to be accountable and to listen carefully to what fellow believers may say about his or her ministry.

But that is only stating it the least complexly. In the New Testament we see that it was the church that set people aside for Christian ministry. They did not usually go off preaching as a result of an individual calling. Study, for example, the sending out of Paul and Barnabas in Acts 13:1–3. We do not read there that the church assented to their missionary journey after Paul and Barnabas had told them what they were going to do in any case. The church was vitally involved in prayer and listening to God from the beginning, and it was out of their worship that Paul and Barnabas were commissioned to Christian service. So the church must be involved in your calling, not as an afterthought, but from the start.

Summing up, there is still a place for a special calling to full-time Christian work, as distinct from the calling that is received by every Christian to serve the Lord. But we have already begun to see that it cannot be undertaken casually. It is a calling to "be set apart for the gospel"; and that makes it a very high calling indeed. It is also one in which the church must be involved. It is not just an individual choice. It is not, then, a question of waking up one morning and feeling that the time has come to do something about your employment prospects, so you wander off down to the nearest job center to see what vacancies they have under the headings of ministry or church work, and apply. It is a calling, not an occupation. If it is a calling, you have to be called. And that leads us to our next question.

HOW DO I KNOW IF I AM CALLED?

One of the distinguishing marks of the great servants of God in the Bible is that they could look back with conviction and say that they had been called by God to speak for him. There the similarity between them ends. Probably with little thought of God, knowledge of being called came for Moses through a burning bush as he was tending sheep. To Elisha it happened as he was plowing a field. For Isaiah it came in the more predictable setting of worship in the temple. For Jeremiah it came when he was young, and he never quite reconciled himself to it. To Peter it came while he was fishing. To Paul it was when he was setting out to persecute the church. God does not seem to be bound by a particular formula or restricted to a special set of circumstances.

The one thing all these and others have in common is that they were sure that God had spoken to them personally and had given them no option but to follow his command and speak for him. The vital ingredient, then, is the note of personal conviction. However it comes and wherever it comes, has God borne in upon you the conviction that you must work for him?

That conviction will probably shape the general direction of your calling, if not the particular form of it. Will it be at home or overseas? Will it be as pastor, evangelist, support worker, or what? That conviction should also discipline you in years to come when you may be tempted to stray from it. That conviction will also prove essential years later as discouragements and pressures arise that entice you into giving up. If God has called, then you can do no other. If it was simply a matter of your own choice, then you are a free agent to do what you like.

Of course, that conviction does not stand alone. It must be understood in the context of the general principles we have already discussed about guidance. Thus, it follows that if it is a genuine call from God, you can generally expect confirmation from three sources. I say "generally" because I am well aware of stories in which the expected confirmation has not been forthcoming and later events have clearly vindicated the person who felt called. Famous preachers have sometimes been turned down by denominational ministerial selection panels, and even more gifted missionaries have been turned down by missionary candidates' boards. Notwithstanding, these are exceptions, and you need to be very careful and very sure before you put yourself in their company.

So what are these three confirmations that you can expect?

First, there is *the confirmation of others in the church*. We have already seen the importance of the role the church has in the matter of calling. Gifts are given by God for the purpose of serving the body of Christ. They are not given to individuals for independent ministry, and still less for ego trips. It is important therefore that fellow members of the body of Christ should be asked how they feel about your calling.

This is not always a simple matter. Some churches are so delighted that at long last, one of their members is going to serve God full-time, that they would gladly support the village dunce if he were to apply! Sometimes churches have little real understanding of what will be involved in Christian service. Sometimes they are just too close, or even related, to the one looking for confirmation and so will find it hard for personal or family reasons to say no even if they have strong reservations. Therefore, try to seek the advice of mature Christian leaders who will be frank and objective in what they say. Do not go only to your friends, whom you know will be enthusiastic.

You are going to need people who can be honest with you. It will spare you much difficulty later on.

Second, there will be *the confirmation of your own gifts.* These will help to show whether the call is appropriate or not. For example, if you are called to be a preacher, are you already being used by God in that way? The question is not if you enjoy it, although that may have some bearing on the issue, but are you being used by God in the sense of being effective? If you believe you are called to be a preacher, are you able to communicate ideas clearly, do people listen with interest, do they invite you back a second time to preach . . . ? These are some of the questions you need to be asking. Of course, you need not have your gift perfectly trained as yet. But there must be evidence in the first place that there is a gift to be trained.

We could paint a similar picture for virtually any task in Christian service. I remember once meeting a person who announced himself as an evangelist employed by a certain church. When I asked him if he had led anyone to Christ, he replied that he did not think so. It struck me as odd that a church should be prepared to employ someone who was not able to give evidence that he was qualified or gifted for the work.

Third, there will be *the confirmation of circumstances.* I readily accept that this may not always be so, and yet normally we should expect circumstances to support your calling. It is unlikely that God will be calling you overseas if you have an elderly parent suffering from a terminal illness dependent on you. It is unlikely that God will be calling you to undertake a four-year training course at your own expense if you have a wife and five children to support. God would seem to have given you other responsibilities and a prior calling in which he wants to find you faithful.

That does not mean to say that if your calling is from God, your circumstances should enable you to enter Christian work with perfect ease and at no cost to yourself. There may well be some very real costs that you have to meet. For many, myself included, it has meant financing oneself through Bible college, without the aid of a grant, by selling a car or property one had come to depend on and love. For others it has meant separation from their wives during a course of training. Hardships there may be. In fact, they may well be the best part of the training course as they lead to the discovery of God's faithfulness and to a learning and self-understanding that would otherwise be lacking.

In spite of that, in general terms, circumstances must still be taken into account, and we should expect them to give us the freedom to move toward the goal God has set before us.

WHAT SHOULD I AVOID?

It would be good if it were otherwise, but to be honest, people do not always enter Christian service for the purest of motives nor in the wisest of ways. The "call" can sometimes be used as a means of solving problems and of furthering ambitions. The process of assessing whether or not you are called to full-time Christian work must include an honest facing up to these ulterior motives and hidden pitfalls. If you do not face them for yourself, it is likely that some selection panel or other will do so for you. And that can be much more painful.

Among those offering themselves for Christian service, several recurring problems and inadequate motives can be identified.

Escapism

Some view going off to Bible college or full-time Christian work as a way of escaping from uncomfortable circumstances at home or work. For some it may be the only acceptable way to leave home and its perhaps unsatisfactory relationships. For others it is a way of running away from failure at work, or from a boring and unsatisfying job, or uncomfortable relationships in the factory or office. For others it is the answer to their unemployment. They cannot get a job, so why not go to Bible college?

Of course God can and does use all these dissatisfactions as incentives to spur some to leave where they are and move into Christian service. The rise in unemployment in recent years has opened up a whole new army of people available for Christian work, but we need to be very careful that such circumstances are a genuine stimulus from God. Not infrequently the desire for Christian work that arises in such circumstances is pure escapism. God's calling is often for his people to stay within such circumstances and learn how to work through them with his grace. Being a Christian does not mean that we should expect a life that is easier for us than for others. So hardship at home, toughness at work, and the plague of unemployment are likely to be our experience as much as that of the unbelievers. He sends the rain on the just and the unjust alike. It is in our weakness that we must learn his strength (2 Corinthians 12:9).

Romanticism

We need to be realistic about the nature of Christian work—and a good many people are not! The problem is that only the tip of Christian ministry is visible, and like the proverbial iceberg, it is the tip that is not seen that is really important. The visible tip includes days of exciting ministry like Keswick or Campus Crusade, or of exciting evangelistic missions when people seem to respond in droves, or even special days of answered prayer and miracles, but what lies behind them?

There are many days in any ministry or mission work that are as routine and boring as in any job—days so discrete and full of interruptions that when you come to the end of them, you feel you have achieved nothing. There are days when everyone you want to visit is out. There are days, sometimes weeks and months, when nothing seems to be happening. There are days when too much is happening, when the telephone never stops, when everybody is shouting at you for something or other, and when the pressure is really on. There are days of discouragement and ordinariness as well as days of sheer inspiration. Do not make the mistake of judging full-time Christian work on the basis of your participation in a short-term mission. Long-term, it can be quite different. Be realistic!

Dishonesty

Dishonesty about ourselves is one of the devil's most common traps for those entering Christian work.

There are many who long to enter Christian work because it will give them status and power and would do wonders for their self-esteem. On the one hand, it ought to be easier to enter the leadership ranks of the church than of secular society. We do not judge leaders by the same standards. We are looking for spiritual gifts not human qualifications. Nevertheless, it has sometimes been too easy to enter Christian work, and there are a number of people as ministers of churches, on the mission field, or in responsible positions in parachurch organizations who would have sunk without a trace in secular work. They have become big fish in a very small pool, and they chose that pool because they wanted to be big. We must be sure before applying for Christian service that we are not seeking power for ourselves and using it as a means for enhancing low self-esteem, or dealing with personal inadequacy, or of providing what we think we have been cheated out of by the world.

The lure of training, qualifications, and title also sometimes makes us less willing to listen to others and assess ourselves objectively as we should. We need to remain teachable and open to direction. This may lead us to dealing with some of our personal problems in other ways than by sublimating them in Christian work.

Guilt

Our world is full of immense need. Everywhere you look there is the need for missionaries, for evangelists, for health specialists, teachers, and farmers. But the need never constitutes the call. It is easy to respond emotionally when you have heard some desperately pathetic picture of people presented at the missionary meeting and feel that you must say, "Here I am, send me." That may be the way God is calling you. But often it will not be so. Often you will be moved by one need this week and another quite different need the following week. Each situation will be equally worthy of your gifts. How are you to decide? You will need a more foundational calling from God than simply responding to a need, however much that may come into the picture.

Haste

Many feel an urgency about Christian service. They believe that the needs of the world will not wait, they have not got time to waste, and Christ might return at any moment—that they must enter now, sometimes even without the necessary preparation and training. But both Scripture and experience suggest we should not be so hasty.

Scripture shows us a God who takes time to mold his workers. Moses was forty years in the desert before being called back to center stage. The disciples were schooled for three years by Jesus before the Day of Pentecost. Paul spent three years in Arabia (Galatians 1:17–18) before presenting himself at Jerusalem. Later he taught Timothy that it was wrong to put young Christians into positions of leadership within the church (1 Timothy 3:6). Apparently God is rarely in the hurry that we are in.

Experience backs up the lesson. Those who rush in often do not stand the test of time, and many fall by the wayside. There is great value in exposing yourself to short-term experience without delay, but if it is a lifetime's ministry you are entering then careful preparation is wise. It lets the root go down and lets the timber be seasoned so that it will stand the test of all the weather conditions it will be exposed to.

Self-sufficiency

You should only move forward in partnership with your church. We have already alluded to some of the reasons for doing this. They can probably assess your gifts better than you can. They are the rightful ones, according to Acts, to take the initiative in commissioning Christian workers. They will be the ones providing support—financial, prayerful, and emotional—and it is only right that they should be asked before you make any moves. They might also have principles and procedures for handling those who are applying for Christian work that you do not yet know about, for the simple reason that you have not needed to know up to now. Therefore, walk in fellowship with others. You cannot expect to be respected as a leader in the church unless you have first learned to be a member of the church and show respect yourself to those over you in the Lord.

HOW SHOULD YOU MOVE FORWARD?

Assuming that you have a right understanding of yourself, have conscientiously faced the pitfalls and temptations, and are openly discussing the situation with others, what should you do next?

Inform Yourself

Take all the steps you can to find out about future opportunities. Before you even write off for details about Bible or theological colleges, find out all you can about the area of work you feel you may be called to. If it is a particular area of the world, who works there, and what do they do? If it is to offer yourself as a farmer, who needs farmers? If you are called to ministry, what are the specific denominational requirements you will have to meet? Or how do parachurch societies work: Who does what, what are their needs, and what training do they require?

Christian magazines, missionary publications, those already in Christian work, and conferences are great sources of information. Start buying them, reading them, talking with them, and attending them! On this basis you can then begin to envisage what sort of training might be appropriate, and then you can start writing to Bible colleges or other suitable establishments. The same sources are likely to give you the addresses you will need.

This may sound very basic and it is! But a surprising number of people I have spoken with, to whom it has not occurred to take these elementary steps, want to enter Christian work. They seem to think there is some computer somewhere in which they can insert their personal details and be told what to do without having to think about it or take any active steps for themselves—sometimes it is sheer laziness. It does not bode well for future Christian service if you cannot be bothered to find out now for yourself about the sort of work in which you might eventually engage.

Keep Praying

To begin with, you may be convinced you have a call but it may not be very specific. Pray that God will not only keep confirming the call but make it increasingly specific. At first you may only be aware that it is a call to work overseas. Through the obtaining of information and the practice of prayer, look to God to refine it so that you can narrow down where, overseas, and in what capacity. Ask God for an increasingly specific burden for a particular people.

You may feel it is simply a call to work at home. Great. But is it to be an evangelist, teacher, pastor, or what? It matters because the way of going about fulfilling your calling will vary according to what that calling is. You need not have it all worked out to begin with. God often does lead a step at a time, but you must have some guidelines or you will not know how to train. Training for Christian service is as diverse as training for medicine. If one went to a career counselor and said he or she wanted to be a medic, one of the first questions to answer would be, What sort of medic? The path to becoming a doctor is different from that of becoming a nurse; that of a dentist different from an occupational therapist; that of a physiotherapist different from that of a veterinary surgeon, but they all work within the field of medicine. So it is with Christian work. Try to be as specific as possible by the time you apply to college, without being so rigid that God cannot surprise you or change your course in the light of what you will experience.

Get Experience

Before applying to college, or to the society of your choice, get as much relevant experience as you can. If you want to be a preacher, join a local preacher's society and make yourself available for smaller churches. If you want to be an evangelist, then go on summer missions and use every opportunity your home church gives you to knock on doors or preach in the open air. If you are called to serve overseas, start attending the appropriate missionary society's conference and prayer days now. Do not wait!

You do not suddenly become a missionary or a pastor once you have finished college and been commissioned or ordained. You must be growing in your experience and gifts from the moment you sense the call onward. If you have no love for people now, you will not find it once you become a "Rev." If you are not interested in the work of missions now, it is a bad recipe for seeking to be employed by one! Gain as much experience as you can.

Build Relationships

We have already mentioned that the ongoing support of people in your church is going to prove vital in years to come. It may be that you will face some hefty bills for your training, or that you have to raise a fair amount of your financial support before the missionary society will send you overseas. And you are likely to present your church with at least some of the bill. In addition, you will need people committed to you in prayer. You will also want, if you serve at a distance, those lovely homey and newsy letters to be sent to you to keep you in touch and affirm that you are remembered. But you can only expect that to happen if you build relationships with people while you have an opportunity to do so.

If you have not attended, prayed with, and served alongside others in your church's activities and thus gotten to know people, you cannot expect them to be supportive of you when you need them. It is a worthwhile investment to give them time and to serve them now. It will pay dividends in the future. You should also take this course because it is right to do so, not just for ulterior motives!

Accept Training

An ancient preacher, John Chrysostom, used a picture of a sea captain to emphasize the need for training for

Christian service. Let me update his picture. If you were asked to pilot an airplane from here to New York, you would refuse, or at least I hope you would. If asked why you had refused, you would reply that you were not trained as a pilot and that the aircraft would not be safe in your hands. The aircraft itself would be an expensive loss were you to wreck it on the runway. But there would also be the more significant question of the lives of the people on board and all the cargo. You dare not risk being put in control of something so valuable without the necessary skill and training. In this case, we are only dealing with a matter of material goods and physical life. How much greater is the obligation, then, asks the twentieth century version of Chrysostom, to train to fly a spiritual plane (usually called "the church") that is full of a cargo of eternal worth? Put in this light, it is easy to understand why training is considered important.

It never ceases to amaze me that people are prepared to invest years in training for ordinary occupations but do not see the need to train for the ministry of God's Word to God's people, or for service through those people to God's world. Careful preparation seems even more important.

BEGIN NOW

Begin preparation for the eventual fulfillment of your call right now. From the time of initially receiving a call you must consider yourself a person-in-training.

If Still in School

Work hard to lay a good foundation of study, according to the abilities and capacities God has given you. It will prove beneficial later. A careful choice of subjects may help. Subjects like English Literature, history, or languages, however, are certainly an advantage, but you must balance them against science or technical subjects that may be even more useful overseas if you envisage using a particular skill like medicine or construction.

If at Work

Use all the opportunities your work naturally provides for you to equip yourself so that when the day comes for entering Christian work you will do so as a person with broad experience and as one who has been matured by the demands of a secular job.

In addition, you might consider also starting to prepare more seriously for Bible college by undertaking some more formal Bible study course by correspondence or through evening classes. That would help to lay a foundation for any course you subsequently might undertake full-time. Life is busy, and there may not be time for study as well as the already competing demands of work, family, and service in the church. You must be the judge, but whatever you decide be sure to keep your long-term goal of Christian service in sight and let that determine and shape how you spend your time in the present.

Whether at School or Work

Remember that what you do now counts because of what it says about you. You may consider it only a preliminary to the real thing, but it is important. The way you tackle it reveals whether you are fit material for Christian service. The Bible teaches "Whatever you do, work at it with all your heart, as working for the Lord, not for men . . . It is the Lord Christ you are serving" (Colossians 3:23–24). It further teaches that unless God can see that he can trust you in the small and the material responsibilities he has given you, he is unlikely to trust you with larger, or spiritual responsibilities (Luke 16:10–12).

To be in Christian service is a tremendous privilege, and is full of exciting opportunities. Also, since it is such a high calling, it carries with it the responsibility to enter with caution, taking care over our guidance and making the approach with a teachable spirit and with a willingness to engage in careful preparation. If these steps are taken, then we can be sure that the God who guides will remain close by our side and in all the changing fortunes and experiences of serving him he will never leave us nor fail us.□

Chapter 10

Guidance for Formation Flying

It is not only individuals who need guidance. The church as a corporate body is constantly in need of guidance too. Should they go in for a rebuilding project? Should they plant a new church? Should they change the format of their services? Should they ordain women? Should they add to their staff? Should they close this group, or change the time of their prayer meeting? And so the discussion continues.

The question of guidance has become more pressing for the church in view of the rapid pace of change that both surrounds us in the wider world and affects us within our own community life. If things were not changing so rapidly, we would not need to be asking the questions and seeking the answers so urgently.

AN OBSOLETE METHOD OF GUIDANCE?

We may look back with some envy on the early days of God's people. When they faced questions and sought guidance, they consulted the high priest who used the Urim and Thummim to provide the answer (Numbers 27:21). We cannot be sure exactly how the Urim and Thummim worked. We know that they were two stones kept in the breast pocket of the high priest's ephod (Exodus 28:30). They must either have been two different colors or both colored differently on each side. When a question was asked, he would either pick out one, the color of which would determine whether the answer was yes or no, or throw them like dice to see on which side up they landed. The latter seems more likely since we know that people did not always get a clear answer (1 Samuel 28:6), which suggests that one stone might land on one side and the other on the opposite side, causing the colors to cancel each other out.

The Urim and Thummim seem to have been a form of casting lots (Proverbs 16:33). If so, it was a method that the early church still used in some form or another when they chose Matthias to fill the place left vacant among the apostles by the desertion of Judas (Acts 1:26). The fact that we never hear of Matthias again has led some to say they were wrong to have used that method. The Bible itself makes no such comment and some church traditions today, like that of the Mennonites, still use the drawing of lots as a way of determining God's decision in the choosing of leaders.

It does seem significant, however, that we never read of the early church's using the drawing of lots again to find out God's will. From the Day of Pentecost they seem to have operated on a different basis. Urim and Thummim guidance was mechanical. With the giving of the Holy Spirit there was no longer any need to resort to these external means of guidance because he was within and among his people. The promise of the new covenant had been fulfilled and its claim that God would "put my law in their minds and write it on their hearts" (Jeremiah 31:33) had become a reality.

FOLLOW YOUR LEADERS?

Even before the Day of Pentecost, the use of the Urim and Thummim had died out. Its role had been taken by the prophets. "Surely," Amos said, "the Sovereign LORD does nothing without revealing his plan to his servants the prophets" (3:7). These, together with the other pastoral leaders of Israel, the priests, and the wise men were looked to for direction. Is not this still, some would ask, the way in which God guides his church today? Do not the prophets and other spiritually gifted leaders have a vital role in determining questions of guidance?

A quick look at the New Testament seems to suggest this is so. Let's review the evidence:

It was through the ministry of the prophets that Paul and Barnabas were sent out on their first missionary tour (Acts 13:1).

Paul appointed leaders in the churches he founded (Acts 14:23) and did not wait for them to appoint their own.

Agabus gave Paul directions about his future (Acts 21:10–14); although, as we have seen, this incident is problematic if we want to make out a case for the authority of prophets from it, since Paul ignores Agabus's advice.

Subsequently, we note that Paul could give clear directions to the churches that he had founded as, for example, in 1 Corinthians 5:3–5; 7:10.

There is a readily recognized place for the prophets in the early church (1 Corinthians 14:1–5, 29–33) although, again, there is a problem. The place they are assigned is specified in terms of "strengthening, encouragement and comfort," not as answering questions of guidance that the church faces.

The later role of elders specifies that they must "direct the affairs of the church" (1 Timothy 5:17), and some would say that their job description would have included not just the spiritual oversight of the church but giving direction over many of the practical issues of church life as well.

Thus, there seems to be a role for leaders in touch with the Holy Spirit to give clear guidance to the church over decisions it has to make. Does that not then settle the issue? God guides through leaders, and it is the job of the rest of the church to concur with what they decide.

Not quite. A fuller study of the New Testament pattern suggests that although they have a vital role to play, they do not have an exclusive role in determining the church's guidance. Other factors must be borne in mind.

Note, for instance, that their role is not a fixed one. There is no clear blueprint nor elder's handbook that stipulates exactly where their authority and its boundaries lie. There is a fluidity of structure and approach. The situation changes as the needs of the time change. Decision making is flexible—first, God directing through one and then another.

Furthermore, none of these leaders are ever presented as infallible. They are never in an unquestionable position. The apostles are closely interrogated by the church as both Acts 6:1–6 records, and the whole of 1 and 2 Corinthians painfully confirms. Paul himself is clearly anxious to distinguish between what is revealed to him by God and what is his own, albeit worthwhile, opinion (1 Corinthians 7:12). The prophets have their words weighed and occasionally ignored (1 Corinthians 14:30). The elders can only expect to be followed as far as they earn and maintain the respect of their people through the spiritual qualities they display.

More important still, the picture the New Testament paints of the early church is not of a great hierarchical organization in which decisions are handed down from above, as if it were the Marine Corps, but of a community in which every member matters and has something to contribute. The dominant perspective is not of leaders pronouncing but of members discussing. We see it in Acts 6 when they appointed deacons; in Acts 15 when they decided on the validity of evangelizing Gentiles; and equally in 1 Corinthians 5 when Paul, having told the church very forcefully what he believed they should do about a certain problem, said it was the church "assembled in the name of our Lord Jesus" who should take action. Elsewhere we get the vivid impression of the early church as a community buzzing with discussion through which they enabled one another to work out the meaning of discipleship and the mind of Christ for their corporate life.

There is an important reason that this should be so and why we should guard this liberty very carefully today. The gospel invites people to freedom (Galatians 5:1), not to a new form of slavery. It is about ordinary persons, just as they are, being heard and understood by God. It is about the burden of authoritarianism being lifted from them. It is about cutting loose from man-made rules and regulations. And that must be reflected in the way in which the church lives its common life as much as in the way individual Christians are called to live.

The wisdom of leaders is a vital ingredient in the church's decision-making process—but it is not the only one. The New Testament cannot be used to argue that the church should abdicate its responsibility of decision making to leaders (and then blame them when it goes wrong!). The fuller picture shows that the whole church must be involved in the process. Therefore, whether it be popes who claim infallibility, councils that dictate, local leaders who direct, or charismatic prophets who say, "Thus says the Lord . . . ," the church must never exempt itself from being part of the process of discerning God's guidance.

ANATOMY OF DECISION MAKING

In view of the importance of the role of the people in coming to decisions, it is worth looking in depth in

Acts 15 at the one detailed record we have of their doing so. The issue that they discussed was fundamental. In what was an unexpected development, Gentiles were being converted. Many doubted whether this should have occurred, but even if they did not question the legitimacy of the whole enterprise, they still had to face the practical problems associated with their conversion. Was it necessary to be circumcised to become a Christian? How much of the law of Moses did a convert have to accept to be an authentic born-again believer? At stake was the very identity of the Christian faith itself. Was it a sect within Judaism, or was it something altogether different?

You can imagine the emotions it generated. It was a debate between the lunatic fringe and the chosen frozen. Strict Jews who had devoted their lives to the study of the Scripture, who were devoted to the traditions of temple and synagogue and led rigid and sober lives, were suddenly asked to accept Gentiles— whose backgrounds were totally different, whose traditions were pagan, and whose lifestyles could only be described as loose—as brothers and sisters in Christ. Surely this could not be right? Surely, the Gentiles had to conform? Surely they had to adopt at least some of the Jewish culture if they were to be Christians, didn't they?

The debate takes us to the heart of many debates churches are having today. As a generation of people are being converted who have not grown up in the church, whose lifestyle has been anything but "Christian" as we popularly understand it, and who are ignorant about the traditional culture of the church, what are we to do? "Make them conform," cries one lobby. "Accept them," cries the other, "as they are." And temperatures rise as questions of what people wear, whether they keep quiet in church, how much they attend, whether they sing hymns to organs, or songs to guitars and drums are all furiously debated. It seems that Acts 15 may have something important to say.

Six guidelines can be discovered here.

The Value of Discussion, verses 5–7

"Then some of the believers who belonged to the party of the Pharisees stood up and said, 'The Gentiles must be circumcised and required to obey the law of Moses.' The apostles and elders met to consider this question. After much discussion . . . "

They confronted the issue instead of sweeping it under the carpet. They saw no problem with airing an issue raised not by the leadership but by others, over which there might be argument and disagreement. They did not consider it a lack of spirituality to share opposing opinions and viewpoints and to use debate as a method by which they could come to a consensus as to the will of God.

Some today are more fearful. To question some leaders is considered a sign of backsliding, or to think differently is treated as a sign of rebellion. Others consider it all a waste of time and forge on ahead in Christian service without ever stopping either to question what they are doing or to gain the support of others in doing it.

The manner of Christian discussion and debates should be different from those in the secular world. We have no right to put people down or suspect people's motives, as often happens outside the church. Rather, the stringent application of love that Paul details in 1 Corinthians 13 should apply to our discussions. Nevertheless, talking together and openly airing our differences is a right and proper way to proceed.

The Importance of Testimony, verses 8–12

Central to the course of discussion were the testimonies given by Peter and by Paul and Barnabas as to what God had done through their ministry and how he had sent signs confirming that the Gentiles, without circumcision, were just as acceptable to him as were the Jews, with their circumcision.

It is important to note the solid content of these testimonies. None of them were of the "I think that . . ." variety. They were not sharing their own personal opinions. They were confident that they had seen God at work, and it was his unmistakable handiwork that they called on the church to recognize. The evidence of what they had to say in terms of the progress of the gospel and of changed lives was available for all to see.

Too often our discussions neglect this dimension. They revolve around our wants, prejudices, or traditions, and God hardly gets a look in.

The Significance of Doctrine, verse 11

Peter's testimony stood the test of sound doctrine! He could tell the assembly that he believed that God had acted in this way because it was the outworking of fundamental doctrine. In his case it was the doctrine of grace. People were not made acceptable to God through their own merits or by their own works but through the gift of the Lord Jesus. From this it followed that Gentiles who had not obeyed the law and undertaken certain rituals were just as acceptable to God as those who had. To argue otherwise would have been to pull the rug out from under the feet of those who preached grace.

Doctrine goes hand-in-hand with testimony. Would that it were always so today. Not only do many current testimonies lack any doctrine altogether, but many of them are in conflict with fundamental doctrine. They claim things for God, or state that he has done certain things, in flat contradiction to sound doctrine. Many of our discussions leave out any reference to doctrine altogether, but doctrine is a systematic statement of what we believe, and therefore is vitally important. To be cut adrift from the anchor of doctrine is to invite chaos and danger. No wonder we are so much at sea today.

Much of our discussion of worship has failed at this point. They have been discussions of what we like without our making any attempt to relate it to what worship is or what principles God has revealed by which worship becomes acceptable to him. Our discussion ought to make the doctrinal foundations more explicit.

The Touchstone of Scripture, verses 13–18

Toward the end of the debate, James introduces Scripture in a most interesting way. His words indicate that he would not have consented to the position that was emerging if it had not been consistent with Scripture. As it was, "The words of the prophets are in agreement with this . . . ," hence the decision they were reaching had passed the test and could be accepted.

Scripture must be our touchstone, too, but not in any glib, literalist, or proof-text type way. This is what is so interesting about the way in which James uses Scripture. It has to be said that James's use of Amos 9:11–12 is fresh and new. Amos would probably have understood his words to have had a more immediate application than the one James gave to it, but James has been pondering the depth of it, sees a fresh dimension to it, and has a fresh understanding of it in the light of what God was doing in the contemporary church. Here we see the ministry of the Holy Spirit as the teacher of truth (John 16:12–14) at work illuminating Scripture in a new light.

Scripture, then, is not to be used to justify the reactionary or the status quo. It is to be read under the ministry of the Spirit to discern with growing insight how God wants his people to live today. This does not justify reading things into Scripture, and it certainly does not permit an "anything goes" attitude. Rather, it is to recognize that the people of God should always be making progress on their pilgrimage and must humbly admit that they have never "arrived."

Luke T. Johnson, in his book on *Decision-Making in the Church: A Biblical Model*, has expressed it well. He writes, "The words of Jesus and the Scripture are normative for the believers, but in a way that allows deeper understanding. Throughout these accounts the experience of God's activity stimulates the church to reread the Scripture and to discover ever new ways in which God maintains continuity with himself."

The Necessity of Listening, verse 12

"The whole assembly became silent as they listened to Barnabas and Paul...." Would that it were always so! Listening is such an essential ingredient to constructive discussion and for reaching agreement, that it is surprising how poor we are at it. We are, of course, usually too well-mannered to chatter or interrupt others when they are speaking. Nor are many of us in church circles likely to descend to the parliamentary tactics of banter and derision to destroy those who differ from us. We are far too polite to do that! But the absence of such rudeness does not mean that we listen to each other. We can switch off inside without ever publicly betraying the fact.

Listening is a disciplined activity. It means we have to put on one side our desire to speak and to hear someone else out. It involves us in humbly admitting we do not know it all and that others may well have the truth. It requires that we reject the idea that we know what the speakers are going to say before they open their mouths. It insists that we do not force a prejudged interpretation onto their words. It invites us not only to hear the words but to get inside the speakers so that we can grasp the meaning of what is said.

Often we fail to reach agreement in the church because we have neglected the basic discipline of listening, and in that we prove ourselves to be no different from the daily arguments that take place between employers and unions. True listening will often lead us to see that the barriers we thought to exist between people are not there at all—that our "opponents" are often merely using different words to say the same thing we are saying—that we should not have been so fearful but can agree with those with whom we thought we differed, and be led by them into new and exciting discoveries about God.

The Indispensability of Communication, verse 22

Once the decision had been reached, the assembly in Jerusalem decided to write a letter informing others of the decision. To help them know what the position was, Paul and Barnabas, together with others, were asked to take the letter to those areas most concerned with the debate.

"Nobody told us." How often have we heard that said? It is extraordinary how we often fail at this basic point. Decisions have no value unless they are communicated to those whom they concern. Some churches and religious bodies are obsessed with the idea of secrecy, while others suffer from plain bad management. Good decisions are sometimes rendered null and void and all sorts of misunderstandings arise simply because they have not been communicated clearly to those whom they most affect.

These six principles seem to lie at the heart of good decision making in the church and to be the means by which God's people can still expect to be guided. They do not exhaust what could be said about the Council of Jerusalem. The role of leaders perhaps deserves comment, and it is only because the question of leadership was dealt with earlier in the chapter that we have not given further attention to it here. Too, it is evident that although the assembly was an open body with free participation by the members of the church in Jerusalem, it was not leaderless. Peter, Paul, and James all had a significant part to play. James, particularly, seems to have sensed the feeling of the gathering, and voiced it on behalf of all. He did so without being dogged by the parliamentary rules of procedure that so frequently make today's church sound more like a town council meeting than a community of believers. To have a spiritually sensitive and respected person at the helm is extremely beneficial in seeking God's guidance.

Perhaps there is another useful rule of thumb hidden in these verses, to which the church should resort more readily in coming to decisions. James wisely says in his judgment, "We should not make it difficult for the Gentiles who are turning to God" (verse 19). How simple and how spiritual! If only we would adopt that commitment, we would not spend so much time reaching some decisions, and many of those we do reach would be a good deal more radical. Often we live in a church-centered culture with its own programs, procedures, and preoccupations that are so foreign to those outside the church that we are making it difficult for them to turn to God. If we asked of every decision—Will this make it easier for people to come to Christ?—we might find that the question of times of service, styles of worship, maintenance of organizations or buildings would take care of itself.

The church sometimes agonizes too much in seeking God's will. We create a mystique about it and create difficulties that seem absent from the experience of the New Testament church. If we were to adopt their way of reaching decisions, we, too, might be released to get on with the real task of mission.

Michael Griffiths, in his excellent book on the church, called *Cinderella with Amnesia*, remarks that too many of us believe that we are on a solo flight to heaven but unfortunately have to engage in an occasional bit of formation flying. For many Christians the church is not a high priority. We have swallowed the individualism of our generation and transferred it to our Christian life. It is far from unimportant, however, in the mind of God. He has designed it to be not only the primary agent of his kingdom here on earth but also the chief means by which we make progress towards spiritual maturity and achieve readiness for our heavenly goal. Flying together, then, is no optional extra. It is a discipline that becomes crucial. If we are to fly together, we need not only to be guided individually but to be guided corporately. The two are not unrelated. Often God guides the church through individuals. Conversely, God often guides individuals through the church.

The means, then, by which God guides the church are not essentially different from the way in which he guides individuals. Although he can and does use supernatural means to guide his people, he more often uses the gifts that he has entrusted to us. Scripture, convictions, advice from others, circumstances, and signs all have their part to play. But at the heart of the matter is the mind renewed by Christ, thinking issues through—prayerfully and openly before God—and reaching wise decisions. It is in this way that we cease to be horses and mules but "understand what the will of the Lord is." It is in this way "he gives us the desires of our hearts."

Both individually and corporately we can have confidence that our God will guide, using the faculties and abilities he has already trusted to us in creation and renewed in Christ.□

Chapter 11

What If ...?

There is no easy formula we can apply about guidance, so there can be no watertight guarantees about its outcome. Essentially, guidance is about developing our relationship with God, who has promised to guide those who trust him. That certainly involves obeying his laws and discovering what pleases him, for there can be no friendship where there is disobedience. But that still leaves the options wide: It means using his gift of the mind renewed by the Holy Spirit and not ignoring the other resources he has made available, so that with an open and prayerful attitude we might discern his will. Occasionally, too, it might mean being open to be guided by remarkable and supernatural means.

In any case, in the final analysis, it is about relationships—our relationship with God and his with us. In that connection Enoch should serve us as a pattern. With sublime simplicity the Bible says of him that he "walked with God; then he was no more, because God took him away" (Genesis 5:24). He succeeded in doing that in very unconducive surroundings, living, as he was, among a very godless generation. It was no easier for him than it is for us, yet because of his close friendship with God, I doubt whether guidance was too much of a problem for him.

Nevertheless, all relationships involve risks. Things do not always go according to plan, and sometimes cherished hopes are not realized. Sometimes it is all too good to be true. So, what if . . . ? In this final chapter let's look at some further problems with guidance that people face.

WHAT IF I LIKE GOD'S GUIDANCE?

This may seem a very strange place to begin, but it is surprising what a problem it is to many people. There used to be a school of Christian teaching that said if you want to do something, then almost certainly, it is not God's will for you to do it. They said that God would certainly guide you to something you do not like, because only by doing so could he ensure that you were not living in the power of the flesh, and only by doing so could he be sure that you were living sacrificially. In consequence, if you want to be a minister, he would definitely send you to the mission field. If you want to go to Kenya, he would send you to Bolivia. If you want to marry a blond, he would give you a redhead . . .

This has left some Christians feeling deeply uneasy if they actually enjoy their work or their Christian service. All sense of security has been taken from them, and they are left wondering whether they can possibly be "in the will of God" if it is so pleasurable to them. If they enjoy what God has given them, they feel guilty.

Now God may certainly have need to work with toughness in our lives on occasions. Love, if it is real love, must be tough. Discipline, pruning, call it what you will, is a necessary part of the maturing process for most of us. The life of Moses is one illustration among several from Scripture where God had to act in just this tough manner in order to shape Moses into the sort of person he wanted him to be before delivering the children of Israel from bondage in Egypt. Human strategies and ideas had to be drawn out of him before he could be useful to God.

On the whole, however, it would be foolish to claim that God always works like this. He is the great and wise Creator who has generously built massive resources into our world and wonderful skills and features into our lives. God knew how he would use us when he formed us (Psalm 139:14–16; Jeremiah 4), and surely often allows the bud of natural interests, inclinations, and character to blossom more fully after our conversion, albeit refined by the Holy Spirit. He does not ride roughshod over his creation, nor is he profligate with his gifts.

There is no sense in God's forcing square pegs into round holes. Not only does that cause discomfort to the peg and the hole, but it almost certainly is an inefficient way of achieving an objective. Greater effectiveness is achieved by matching the peg to the hole. So it is in our lives. We are likely to be more effective for God not when we are serving him out of a sense of drudgery or obligation, believing that we are in the wrong place, but when we are naturally exploiting the God-given personality and interest that are ours, believing we are in the right place.

Some killjoys in the New Testament were trying to teach that if one were truly following God, one would have to lead a miserable life. But Paul counters them, saying, "Everything God created is good, and nothing is to be rejected if it is received with thanksgiving, because it is consecrated by the word of God and prayer" (1 Timothy 4:4–5). The qualifications are important. They warn us of the danger of taking things for granted, of plowing on ahead with our cherished plans without reference to God. If we do so, then we shall almost certainly run into problems. We can have stubborn and foolish wills, thus, as the potter does on the clay, God may well need to exercise discipline to create something fitting out of our flawed lives. Giving us answers we do not like and leading us in paths we would not choose may well be his way of doing so, but we must not throw the baby out with the bathwater. There may well be some dangers in presuming that we should enjoy what God tells us to do but more often than not, since he is a loving and gracious Father, that is exactly what we shall probably experience.

Paul gives us other clues as to why this must be. In Philippians 2:12 and 13 he writes, "Work out your salvation with fear and trembling, for it is God who works in you to will and to act according to his *good* purpose" (emphasis mine). In Romans 12:2 he writes of God's will (meaning probably moral will, but by implication it concerns God's total design for our lives) as "good, pleasing and perfect." His purpose for us is *good*. Do not be casual about it. But do be confident and thankful. And enjoy it, without guilt.

WHAT IF I DO NOT LIKE GOD'S GUIDANCE?

Such happiness is not everybody's experience, and there are some who do not like the way God has led them. They desperately long to marry, but remain single—are willing to serve overseas but are stuck in boring jobs at home. They are free to do anything, yet have no choice about it because they must look after elderly parents . . . and so on. How do we explain and handle these disappointments?

Because there is no single answer to these varied discontents, which answer or combination of answers applies to you if you find yourself in this situation is something you yourself must work out, perhaps with mature pastoral help.

To begin with, some desires are just plain wrong. The discontent is caused not by not getting what you want but by your wanting it in the first place. Your ambitions and desires are not sufficiently in tune with God's revealed moral will or his personal spiritual agenda for you. To want to marry someone who is already married to someone else is wrong. To stake your hopes on gaining material acquisitions is also wrong. There is no shortcut to contentment. The answer lies in repentance, which means, literally, changing your mind. Contentment lies in giving up what is wrong and in learning both to desire and do what is right. Because our minds have been renewed by the Spirit, we are to put off the old self and put on the new self "created to be like God in true righteousness and holiness" (Ephesians 4:22–24).

Not all discomfort, however, can be put down to deliberate sin within our lives. Sometimes it arises from God's desire to mold us even more into his liking. We have seen an illustration of the way he did that in the life of Moses. Hardship, discipline, suffering, deferred or denied wishes, pressures of one sort or another have their value in producing maturity. Paul understood this when he wrote, "We also rejoice in our sufferings, because we know that suffering produces perseverance; perseverance, character; and character, hope. And hope does not disappoint us, because God has poured out his love into our hearts by the Holy Spirit whom he has given us" (Romans 5:3–5).

Consider the labor pains a mother experiences to give birth to a child. It is sometimes the same in our own lives. Labor pains are necessary to produce spiritual life. We make a wrong assumption if we think it is all going to be easy.

On occasion, the discomfort arises from God's discipline in our lives. His discipline, just another aspect of his love, proves that we are his genuine children (Hebrews 12:4–13). The time to worry is when he no longer interposes to discipline us. Perhaps we are growing apart from him or treating holy things too lightly. In such circumstances, to bring us back to himself, God often brings a dissatisfaction with life and a discontent with the things on which we are beginning to rely. The things in our lives that take the place that God should occupy, usually bring no joy. Yet, stupidly, we often fail to recognize this ourselves and need a messenger from God to point it out to us.

The children of Israel were in that situation when they returned from exile and set about building their own houses while leaving God's house still in ruins. The prophet Haggai was sent to explain to them that this was why they planted much but harvested little; ate, but never had enough; drank, yet were always thirsty; earned wages, but seemed to put them into a purse with holes (Haggai 1:6–7). Just as Haggai spoke to his contemporaries for God, so discipline might speak to us if we will only listen.

There is an even deeper reflection on why we sometimes do not like the way we are guided. It is quite simply because we are called to identify with the cross of Jesus. The New Testament never gives a guarantee that life for the Christian will be blissfully happy. Rather, it calls us to take up our cross and follow Jesus. To do this is to engage in a voluntary abandoning of one's own life and concerns and a laying down of one's life for others. Again and again we are called to be united with Jesus in his death if we wish to experience the power of his risen life. The call is basic to our understanding of baptism (Romans 6:3). It was woven into the experience of Paul (2 Corinthians 11:16–13:4). It was central to the preaching of the apostles (Galatians 2:20; Philippians 3:10).

To move beyond the Cross to resurrection requires that we first of all accept the Cross. Unless we willingly go to Calvary, we will not find our way to the empty tomb. The answer to our dislike of the way we have been guided, therefore, rarely lies in struggling and protest. As with Jesus, it usually lies in acceptance. From that death, that acceptance, new possibilities and new life arise.

Pastoral experience underlines that this is wise and good theology. Those who refuse to accept the way they have been guided and continue to kick against it usually continue to be restless and discontented. Those who reconcile themselves to their limitations and disappointments often find release and meet unexpected new opportunities. Hence, the wisest advice of all when it comes to guidance we do not like is to accept it.

WHAT IF I STILL DO NOT KNOW WHAT TO DO?

There are some people who are natural ditherers and who never seem able to come to a decision. They apply all the lessons and still get nowhere. Others find themselves in this situation occasionally even though it might be quite uncharacteristic of them. What are such people to do?

The important thing is to understand that the damage caused by not making a decision is often far worse than any potential damage involved in making the wrong decision. An old management adage, while not infallible, often applies: "Almost any decision is better than no decision." When no decision is reached, opportunities are missed, people are inconvenienced (or treated with discourtesy as beings that have no feelings and need no answers), foundations are not laid, and life is left suspended in limbo.

If it is a defect of character, you need to ask others to come close to you and challenge you to be courageous and make decisions. Then they must stand with you, giving support, as you work through the outcome of that decision, discouraging you from undoing it.

If you fear to make a decision because it might be the wrong one before God, then, providing you have treated the matter conscientiously before him, listen to the voice of Jesus, who often commanded his disciples not to be afraid. Move ahead believing that God is quite capable of redirecting you if you have got the matter wrong. As someone once pointed out to me, it is far easier to change the course of a car that is moving than to turn a car around that is stopped. So it is with guidance. To be on the move in some direction is less of a problem to God than if you are stationary.

In his last book, *The God of Our Journey*, before his premature death, Michael Walker wrote:

> The route of (God's) will might lie through the center of our lives but, if we reject that high calling, he will turn to other ways, explore other possibilities, extend other invitations.
>
> At the heart of all his dealings with us is an eternal lover and an infinite patience. Omniscience could foresee every future decision and omnipotence ensure conformity to God's will. Instead, God calls us into partnership with himself, a partnership in which he accepts all the risks of our humanity.

Do not make yourself bigger than God. You cannot thwart his plan or deny him his will. Therefore, since he is greater than you, even if there is a wrong decision on your part he can either redirect it or triumph over it. So take heart! And make decisions!

There is yet another reason why we sometimes do not decide, and that is because we sometimes think too hard about something. The more introspective we are, the more difficult it is to be certain about anything, especially our motives. I know my wife loves me. The evidence of it is all around me, but it would be possible for me to gnaw away at the question in such a way that I could convince myself that she does not. I could overturn every piece of evidence and explain her actions and emotions in other ways. I could rationalize things . . . such as, she only loves me because she can live in this house that way; she says she loves me but really she has a need for a man in her life, any man would do—and so on. The more I look into the matter, the less certain I can become and the more unreasonable, too! If we are to function at all in life, then there comes a point when we have to believe the plain evidence before us and act upon it. The same is true of guidance.

The wise man who wrote Ecclesiastes understood the tendency in human nature to procrastinate and the folly of so doing. He warned, "Whoever watches the wind will not plant; whoever looks at the clouds will not reap" (11:4). But that is no way to live. Rather, "Sow your seed in the morning, and at evening let not your hands be idle, for you do not know which will succeed, whether this or that, or whether both will do equally well" (11:6). You may not know, but that is no reason for indecision and inactivity. God knows, and that is what counts. So decide, and act, and leave the outcome to him.

WHAT IF IT ALL GOES WRONG?

This is no academic question. It is one that is voiced frequently. A church believes it is led of God to organize an evangelistic mission and does so believing not only that people will be converted but that the necessary finances will be raised. The mission comes and goes, but no one is converted and huge debts are left. Did they get their guidance wrong? A group of people are convinced that for God they must open up a home to minister to needy people. There seem so many confirmations, so they move ahead in spite of not being sure where all the money is coming from. The project fails and they are left with huge debts. Why did God allow it? A church calls an additional staff member, believing that giving will increase to support him, but it does not. Had they made a mistake? A friend moves to a new job, sure it is God's will, but he is only there for a short and unpleasant time before he is fired. Another moves to a new town, believing that God has led him, but he is unable to sell his house and get one in his new location. What went wrong? A Christian worker accepts a new position, convinced that the opportunity is from the Lord. He is only there briefly before he is tragically killed in an accident. Was he right to have made the move?

All these questions have been raised with me in recent days. They are usually asked with both anguish and urgency. What is one to think? What can one say?

To begin with, the fact that the outcome of the decision went wrong may not say anything about whether the decision itself was right or wrong. Within most of us there is a deeply ingrained feeling that if things go wrong, it is because God is punishing us for some wrong we have done or wrong decisions we have made. This may not be so at all. Jesus twice specifically denied that there was any automatic connection between sin and misfortune. The tower of Siloam did not fall and kill eighteen people because they were more wicked than anyone else (Luke 13:4), nor in John 9 had the man healed of his blindness been born blind because he or his parents had particularly sinned. Such disasters and misfortunes happen. They are a sad part of our fallen and twisted world and they always will be until the creation is finally reconciled to God (Romans 8:22; Colossians 1:20). That's life, and Christians are not exempt from it. If the housing market collapses, Christians will not be immune from it. As long as automobile accidents happen, Christians will be caught up in them. Such misfortunes do not necessarily point to anyone getting his or her guidance wrong.

Likewise, many disastrous outcomes can be traced to bad decisions and unrealistic thinking; therefore, it is essential that when things go wrong those involved reflect with real honesty on the process by which they came to the decision and learn from any mistakes made. When new ventures are proposed in a Christian gathering, it takes courage to evaluate them critically and even more courage to oppose them. Those who do are often made to feel that their faith is lacking or that their spirituality is being called into question. Undoubtedly experience suggests that churches are often led down certain paths too uncritically and without subjecting the issue to the sort of examination that they undertook in the early church. What often happens in the absence of genuine discussion of an issue is that people vote for it at the meeting but do not mandate the financial or other needed follow-up support. Consequently, it ends in failure, which can result in great dishonor being done to God's name as projects collapse and bills mount.

It is much better to think clearly, do the homework properly, and prepare the way thoroughly before embarking on a project. Jesus made this point when he said in one of his parables that no one builds a tower without estimating the cost and seeing if he has enough money to complete it, and no king goes to war without first working out his chances of success (Luke 14:25–33). Yet, Christians frequently ignore this simple advice. Jesus also once commented that "the people of this world are more shrewd in dealing with their own kind than are the people of the light" (Luke 16:8). In many decisions greater shrewdness would have been advantageous!

The final word must be a reminder that God is sovereign. He therefore reigns over all, bringing his good purposes about in all the experiences of life, both good and bad, right and wrong. Nevertheless, even if it all seems to have gone wrong, it does not mean that God has abandoned us. Even if the worst happens, he remains a God who is near, a refuge, and a very present help in times of trouble.

We have seen how he did this in the life of Joseph, Moses, and Paul. We have heard the assurance of Scripture that "in all things God works for the good of those who love him, who have been called according to his purpose" (Romans 8:28). Our quiet confidence must lie in the stress given to "all things." The "all" includes the failures, misguided decisions, wrongs, and misfortunes as well as the positive, the successes, and the blessings of life. Therefore, learn the lessons and correct any mistakes, by all means, but do not endlessly speculate on questions that cannot be resolved trying to explain where the blame lies or what went wrong. The task is to rely on God today and to learn to live for him in the present and for tomorrow, no matter how dark today and tomorrow might seem.

Søren Kierkegaard said, "Life can only be understood backwards. The trouble is, it has to be lived forwards." In this life there will always remain deep mysteries and heart-wringing questions. With hindsight we may understand a little more of life's perplexities while on earth. Looking back, we can sometimes see why God allowed things to happen or we can see them fitting into a pattern. Deeper understanding may emerge that helps us to accept the tragedies and failures, but only with the hindsight of heaven will we be able to understand it all.

In the meantime we must trust our lives to the God who guides and who has proved to be a never-failing shepherd to his people. And we must learn to walk with him.☐